TWENTIETH CENTURY
HOLINESS SERMONS

By

Twelve Active Ministers

First Fruits Press
Wilmore, Kentucky
c2016

Twentieth century holiness sermons.
By twelve active ministers.

First Fruits Press, ©2016

Previously published by the Pentecostal Publishing Company, [191-?].

ISBN: 9781621715320 (print) 9781621715337 (digital) 9781621715344 (kindle)

Digital version at http://place.asburyseminary.edu/firstfruitsheritagematerial/129/

For all other uses, contact:

First Fruits Press
B.L. Fisher Library
Asbury Theological Seminary
204 N. Lexington Ave.
Wilmore, KY 40390
http://place.asburyseminary.edu/firstfruits

Twentieth century holiness sermons / by twelve active ministers. Wilmore, Kentucky : First Fruits Press, ©2016.

115 pages, [1] leaf of plates : portraits ; 21 cm.

Reprint. Previously published: Louisville, Ky. : Pentecostal Publishing Company, [191-?].

ISBN - 13: 9781621715320 (paperback)

Contents: I. A scriptural putting / Andrew Johnson -- II. God's call to sinners and believers / A.M. Hills -- III. Consecration to God / R.L. Selle -- IV. A three-word gospel / C.F. Wimberly -- V. Holiness and the church / Joseph H. Smith -- VI. The light of the world / E.P. Ellyson -- VII. The mind of the master / Will H. Huff -- VIII. Perfect love / Clement C. Cary -- IX. A vision of Christ / J.B. Kendall -- X. The danger in neglecting salvation / H.W. Bromley -- XI. Ye must be born again / E.A. Fergerson -- XII. Pentecost and its results / G.W. Ridout.

1. Holiness--Sermons. 2. Sanctification--Sermons. 3. Sermons, American. I. Title.

BT765 .T83 2016   234.8

Cover design by Jonathan Ramsay

asburyseminary.edu
800.2ASBURY
204 North Lexington Avenue
Wilmore, Kentucky 40390

First Fruits
THE ACADEMIC OPEN PRESS OF ASBURY SEMINARY

First Fruits Press
The Academic Open Press of Asbury Theological Seminary
204 N. Lexington Ave., Wilmore, KY 40390
859-858-2236
first.fruits@asburyseminary.edu
asbury.to/firstfruits

1. Rev. Andrew Johnson. 2. Rev. A. M. Hills. 3. Rev. R. L. Selle. 4. Rev C. F. Wimberly. 5. Rev. Joseph H. Smith. 6. Rev. E. P. Ellyson. 7. Rev. W. H. Huff. 8. Rev. C. C. Cary. 9. Rev. J. B. Kendall. 10. Rev. H. W. Bromley. 11. Rev. E. A Fergerson. 12. Rev. G. W. Ridout.

Twentieth Century Holiness Sermons.

By Twelve Active Ministers.

Pentecostal Publishing Company,
Louisville, Ky.

CONTENTS.

20th Century Holiness Sermons.

SERMON I.

A SCRIPTURAL PUTTING.

Rev. Andrew Johnson.

"That ye put off * * * the old man," * * * "That ye put on the new man, which after God is created in righteousness and true holiness." Ephe. 4:22, 24.

Since man by nature is wrong, being tainted and corrupted by the fall, it is the glorious work of grace to bring him back to original righteousness. The fact that he has been utterly deprived of divine life necessitates the entire reconstruction in every phase and feature of the intellect, sensibilities and will. Hence the plan of salvation in the scheme of redemption was devised with reference to the restoration of a lost and fallen race. Poets have written, philosophers have reasoned, and theologians argued concerning this theme of themes. Angels have desired to look into its mysteries and flaming evangels have proclaimed it to the ends of the earth. The greatest and most logical of all the Apostles thoroughly analyzed the subject. Let us observe therefore, how beautifully and tactfully he presents the matter in his Epistles to the churches.

I.   PUT ON.   In Eph. 4:22 he exhorts them to put off the old man and put on the new man.   In Galatians he declared that so many as had been baptized into Christ had put on Christ.   The Romans were admonished to put on the Lord Jesus Christ and not to make provisions for the flesh. These teach that some superior and extraneous force must be brought into requisition.   When the earth, for instance, was a nebulous mass of chaos, it was entirely impossible for it to evolve itself under the action of the centripetal and centrifugal forces, into cosmic symmetry and beauty. The application of an outside or external agency was necessary.

Just so the Eternal Spirit of God must move upon or over the lost soul. A divine element evidently must be introduced, the heavenly exotic must be planted, life from God must be imparted.   Even physical life as we know it, came not, as some agnostics would have us believe, from the sparks of impinging worlds, or the fortuitous concourse of atoms, but through the principle of biogenesis— life from preceding life.

If we examine in connection with this thought the philosophy of the perpetuity of life we   find that even the human body, with all its organic functions and skillful arrangements, cannot extend its existence without constant supplies of rich nourishment appropriated from the external realm.   The mind itself must receive instruction and information by external perception.   The body would dwarf and die, and the mental life fail of development left to themselves. Food for the former and truth for the latter and these supplied by the intervention of externalities, is the law of extended existence in the physical and metaphysical world.

This rule not only holds as intimated above, but applies with double force in regard to the salvation and preservation of the soul. Everywhere in the Bible we are besought to look beyond and above ourselves for the help that was laid upon one that was mighty. Ye must be born from above, is the *sina qua non* of entrance into the kingdom. Every fluttering bird, struggling beast, and sprinkling priest in the old dispensation, representing the necessity of external agency point to Jesus, the antitype by whom and through whom alone we are to receive life and life more abundantly. The dry bones of the valley in Ezekial's vision, rattled, rose and came together at the voice of prophecy, and were bound with sinew and clothed with flesh and yet all this was effected by an external force as was the finishing touch, the gust from the winds of heaven, that gave them life.

Again, it is necessary that the new man (a real principle of divine life) be put on, as formal works and ritualistic services, which are often furnished as substitutes, are not sufficient to regenerate. "Not by works of righteousness which we have done, but according to his mercy he saved us by the washing of regeneration and the renewing of the Holy Ghost" (Titus 3:5). The sculptor may with chisel and hammer, bring the perfection of form from the rough block of crude marble, but he cannot add to the polished piece of statuary, however beautiful he may make it, that indefinable and inestimable boon of real life. Nor can the artistic painter infuse life into his charming production which he throws upon the canvas. However the true objects of which these are but the mere classical shadows, could not depend upon art and skill for existence. Yet the creative genius of the "immortal" artist could as easily and nearly superinduce the essential element of life to his specimens as the priest or preacher could impart divine life around the communion rail or at the baptistry. Forms and ceremonies can never impart the grace which they, in the divine economy, are used to signify. Nothing short of a personal and appropriative contact with divinity will enliven the soul, kindle holy fire upon the altar of the heart, and establish within the individual the principle of life. The new man must be put on the throne of our spiritual nature.

II. PUT UNDER. "I keep under my body and bring it into subjection: lest that by any means, when I have preached to others, I myself should be a castaway" (1 Cor. 9:27). Here is the Scripture that teaches the true doctrine of suppression. What are we to suppress or keep under is the question. The new man is to be put on and the outward man is to be put under—suppressed. What wholesome advice this. There are natural appetites that must be guarded, physical infirmities that need to be watched and legitimate desires to be kept in bounds of temperance. It is the greatest of fallacies to call these things sin, for it is plainly stated in the Bible that every sin that a man doeth is without the body. Our physical members are to be yielded as servants of righteousness unto holiness. The body itself is to be presented a holy sacrifice in order to prove the good, acceptable and perfect will of God. It takes more than the physical and chemical elements that go to make up the external and outermost part of the human organization to constitute sin. The intelligence, motive and will must be brought into play and in them are invested the power to wilfully transgress a known law—to commit sin. The soul that sinneth it shall die. How absurd then that antinomian view that after regeneration the soul cannot sin, but the body sins constantly and necessarily.

There are other teachers who, while they do not claim that the body *per se* commits actual sin, yet contend that sin (inbred) dwells in the flesh (body). According to this theory the atonement is insufficient, the mission of Christ who came to destroy the works of the devil,is a failure. If Satan could inject sin in the body and Christ could not take it out, the whole plan of salvation would come to a halt and the pandemonium of hell would shout the victory over the Lamb.

Such is not possible, for the keys of death and hell and the grave are hanging to the girdle of the King of kings and Lord of lords. Besides the term flesh as used in these connections means the carnal mind. Hence there is no reason in the universe why we should not know the truth which makes us free indeed—free from sin and give us fruit unto holiness.

Let us then as Paul keep our bodies under and bring them into subjection—in other words let us "suppress" them and by so doing impress the world around us that there is a reality in the holiness which we profess. We will have plenty to occupy us in warding the enemy off and subjugating and regulating the outer man without keeping a little supply of sin in some remote corner of our existence, the "suppression" of which is thought to be necessary to give us employment and keep us humble. Therefore put the body under and be not a castaway.

III. PUT OFF. That ye put off concerning the former conversation the old man. Knowing this that our old man is crucified that the body of sin might be destroyed. The Greek word for "put off" is *apotheomai* and the one for destroy in the passage quoted is *katargeo*. The meanings of these words respectively as given by lexical authority are first to *thrust away, to reject*. The second one, to *make idle, to render inoperative, to bring to naught*. In order that we may understand the strength, inten-

sity and nature of these words from the original
describing what must be done with the old man,
let us try them in other passages of Holy Writ,
or rather let us see how the divinely inspired writers employed them. Acts 7:27, But he that did
his neighbor wrong thrust (*aposatoo*) him away.
Acts 13:46. "It was necessary that the word of
God should first have been spoken to you; but seeing
ye put (*apotheisthe*) it from you, we turn to the
Gentiles." Rom. 11:1. "I say then, Hath God cast
away (*aposatoo*) his people? God forbid." 1 Tim.
1:19. "Holding faith and a good conscience; which
some having put away (*apoosamenoi*) concerning
faith have made shipwreck." Rom. 3:3. "Shall
their unbelief (*katargesei*) make the faith of God
without effect?" 1 Cor. 1:28. "And the things
which are not to bring to naught (*katargese*)
things that are." 1 Cor. 2:6. "Nor of the princes
of this world that come to naught" (*katargowme-
non*.)

These instances reveal the potency of the word
for *put off* and also *destroy*. The man who thrust
away Moses certainly did not desire to "suppress"
him as a slave, but with all the earnestness of an
irritated soul, he wished to get rid of him or to
banish him from his presence or absolutely have
nothing in common with him The same is true
in regard to the Jews' attitude toward the gospel
of Christ delivered to them. They utterly ignored
it and rejected it with such emphasis and decision
as to cause the Apostle to leave them and turn to

the Gentiles. This is a case of complete apathy toward and entire separation from something. When the question was asked "Has God cast away his people?" the same word was employed. Here it can mean nothing else than perfect separation from—every bond of union, every cord of attachment forever severed. Of course the reply was negative, but the meaning of the verb could have been no stronger had such been the attitude toward his people. The shipwreck of Hymenaeus and Alexander doesn't favor the theory of the Suppressionists very much, if the old man is to be scuttled, twisted, and torn and smashed like lightning, wind and wave demolishes a ship.

The term destroy speaks for itself. If the old man is crucified that the body of sin might be destroyed, it begins to look as though there is a faint possibility of getting rid of this troublesome "nature." The references from Corinthians are easily understood and are decidedly on the side of the Eradicationist. The strongest word, probably, is the one used in Col. 2:11. "In whom also ye are circumcised with the circumcision made without hands in putting off the body of the sins of the flesh by the circumcision of Christ." It is *apekdusei,* found in no other writer, but only in this passage. The double preposition shows its superlative strength. *Apo* means from *and ek* also means from, both united means "sure enough" from. So if language stands for anything we can be completely cleansed and entirely delivered from the old man or inbred sin in this life and throughout eternity.   Praise God!

The only verse that apparently supports the Keswick side of the question is Heb. 2:14—that through death he might destroy him that had the power of death, that is, the devil.   Hence they would make us mean that God was going to anni-hilate the devil himself.   Of course this view is untenable.   The text evidently means that Christ will destroy or bring to naught the power of the devil who is the instigator of sin, the wages of which is death.   When the last enemy is destroyed and death is swallowed up of life, and the devil cast into the lake of fire and in all the fair realms of heaven and the renewed earth "Sickness, sorrow, pain and death are felt and feared no more," the victory will be complete.   The devil's power in bringing about death will then be fully and forever destroyed.   The only difficulty whatever in the passage is the rhetorical figure, a metonymy, put-ting the cause for the effect.

Since the "old man" can and must be put off in this life, at what particular time it may be asked may this work be accomplished?

As this sin principle of carnal mind cannot be repented of, forgiven, adopted or regenerated, it is safe, reasonable and scriptural and in harmony with experience and consistent with the va-rious creeds of Christendom to say that our complete riddance therefrom is not effected in, by or at the moment of conversion.   Nor will

it do to deny the existence of original sin when it
is so plainly taught, largely admitted, and sensibly felt. Granting, for the sake of argument, that
there is no native depravity, how then can we account for the universality of guilt, the universality of death and the universality of the atonement.
Finney, the great evangelist of yesterday, tried to
account for the universality of guilt by saying it
it was due to free agency in the presence of temptation ,and declared it unphilosophical to look for
another cause when one was found. Philosophy,
it might be replied, does not rest with a *probable*
cause, but searches till it finds the *real* cause.
Some of the theologians(?) of today seem to have
found an entirely new remedy to rid themselves
of depravity. Instead of seeking the blood of
Jesus to *cleanse* it away they have decided to *de-
fine* it away. If ye walk in the light of their theology it *defineth* the soul from all sin. The following are some of their definitions: "Depravity
is an inseparable accompaniment of a life of pro-
bation and attaches to the physical entity." Rather
is it not a separable impediment to a life of regeneration and attaches to the physical being?
"A strong liability to sin." How is that for a
profound definition of carnality? "A keen sus-
ceptibility to temptation." Yet those of the Zin-
zendorfian persuasion, or the one blessingists contend that this is all that remains in the heart of
the truly regenerated. However, Paul in the third
chapter of 1 Cor. calls it carnality. "I brethren,

could not speak unto you as unto spiritual, but as
unto carnal, even babes in Christ. I have fed you
with milk and not with meat, hitherto ye were not
able to bear it, neither yet now are ye able, for ye
are yet carnal." They were babes in Christ, certainly regenerated, still they were carnal. It is claimed by one, high in authority, that these Corinthians were not normal in their regeneration, giving
us another definition of carnality, perchance the
"abnormality of regeneration"—they were not in
the highest enjoyment of regeneration, we admit.
They were certainly in Christ, and must have been
in a state of normal regeneration when they first
entered that state, but at that time they were carnal, otherwise the apostle should have said ye are
again carnal instead of ye are *yet* carnal.

Once more, it is claimed that if people can be
cleansed from all inbred sin in this life their pos-
terity would be born pure. If the parents are
holy the children will not be possessed with inbred sin. That may sound plausible and there
is more sound than sense in it. "But wilt thou
know O vain man," that superinduced qualities are
not transmitted by natural generation. It is not
a fact in nature that qualities are transmitted by
those who do not possess the qualities through
whom or which they are transmitted. The immediate parentage of a black lamb may be white. Holiness in the parents of the child was acquired by
a special act of faith on the part of the individual
and is not transferable. The presence of this holi-

ness in their hearts expels sin. Holiness is not
extended in this form to the child, hence there is
nothing of the acquired nature of holiness in its
heart. The absence of holiness therein opens the
gate for the presence of inbred sin, as all must
have one or the other. The parents being unable
to transmit their acquired holiness and not having
inbred sin they could not in the regular, direct and
immediate way transfer that. The geneological
inheritance of the child accrues from a more remote ancestry even from Adam.

The new man, therefore, must be put on, the
outward man must be put under, the inward man
put right, and the old man put off; hence *the
Scriptural putting.*

SERMON II.

GOD'S CALL TO SINNERS AND BELIEVERS.

Rev. A. M. Hills.

> "Submit yourselves therefore to God. Resist the devil, and he will flee from you. Draw nigh to God and he will draw nigh to you. Cleanse your hands, ye sinners; and purify your hearts, ye double minded." James 4:7, 8.

There are two great moral forces in the Universe. There are two great supreme leaders—only two. There are only two kingdoms,—the kingdom of light and the kingdom of darkness. None of us can be indifferent spectators of these rival powers, for we are subjects of the one or the other. There is no neutrality. We must follow one of the two commanders named in the text. We are the prizes for which they contend in ceaseless warfare.

"The soul of man, Creator's breath,
   Which keeps two worlds at strife;
Hell moves beneath to work its death,
   And heaven to bring it life."

I. Notice the sublime, God-given power of the human will. Hear these sharp commands that ring out like the crack of a rifle. "Submit," "re-

sist," "draw-nigh," "cleanse," "purify," "be-af-
flicted," "humble-yourselves." There is not a
hint here at Calvinistic, "moral inability," either
in *saint* or *sinner*. Neither is there any sugges-
tion here that some day God will come to the elect
with a sovereign, irresistible grace, and surely in-
fallibly convert them. This is in some creeds and
theologies; but it is not in the Bible.

No, the Infinite God calls upon man to bestir
himself, awake out of the stupid sleep and carnal
security of sin, yield his obstinate will, go out of
the sinning business, and "submit to God." He is
commanded, just *as* he is and *where* he is, to cease
running after the devil and "draw nigh to God."
There is not a hint of any inability to obey.

O, men coddle themselves. They play the baby
act. They excuse themselves for their wickedness
by denying their *ability* to quit sinning. Such
talk insults conscience, denies consciousness and
mocks God.

When Finney was a young, unconverted lawyer,
he attended a Presbyterian church. His pastor
would preach about repentance, urge the duty to
repent upon the congregation. But he would invariably close by telling the congregation that
none of them were able to repent until God was
pleased in His own time to give them the ability
and the irresistible grace. Again he would preach
on faith and the duty to believe in Jesus and be
saved; and close by telling them that none of
them could believe until God gave them the abil-

ity and the irresistible grace. Of course, then the
elect could not help repenting and believing and
being saved. Moreover, all the non-elect must go
to hell because of the lack of ability and irresistible grace.

To the astute, legal, logical mind of Finney,
the absurdity of such preaching was next to infinite. And no wonder, for it makes God directly
responsible for all the unrepentance and sin of
our wicked race. How utterly false such teaching is our text clearly indicates.

II. The text shows that the devil can be suc-
cessfully RESISTED. No man need serve him. "The
way of the transgressor is hard," but no man is
compelled to walk in it for lack of ability to resist the devil and get out of it. We do not need to
be dragged into sin or corralled into hell. The
devil is mighty; but he cannot conquer us in a
fair fight. He is compelled to resort to "DEVIC-
ES." Any man can rise up in his God-given
might and vanquish Satan and all the imps of
hell. If a man sins it is because he chooses to.
If he goes to hell, it is by his own consent.

Then, O man, "Awake to righteousness, and sin
not!" Arouse you! Shake yourself, like Samson
in his chains and break away from the toils of Satan. "Resist the devil and he will flee from
you."

III. "Draw nigh to God." By your own choice
of soul, tear away from Satan, run towards God
and cry for His help.

1. "Submit." Throw up your hands in unconditional surrender, and God will make peace with your soul. Ground your arms of rebellion, and consent to the government of 'God that it is holy and to the divine law that it is good. Own up before the Universe that "the judgments of the Lord are true and righteous altogether."

2. With all your sins and the story of your shame on your lips, run to His bosom, and His heart will be drawn toward you. The parable of the Prodigal Son is a picture of God's willingness to receive any repentant child. The ring of adoption and the robe of grace and the feast of pardoning love, and the Father's smile of reconciliation await any sinner who will only turn to God.

IV. "Cleanse your hands, ye sinners." The hands represent the *doing*, the voluntary deeds of men. To cleanse the hands is to forsake sin. The prophet Daniel said to Nebuchadnezzar: "Break off thy sins by righteousness, and thine iniquities by showing mercy to the poor."

Again, to cleanse the hands is to get justified from the guilt of sin, the liability to punishment. It is to be pardoned and made at peace with God. It is to have the conscience made clean by the cleansing blood. It brings peace of soul to David after the commission of adultery and murder. It makes Peter comfortable after his wicked cursing and cowardly denial of his Lord. It will bring a sense of peace with God to any sinner's heart.

V. "Purify your hearts, ye DOUBLE-MINDED."

Who are double-minded people? Surely the sinner is not. He has "the carnal mind which is enmity against God." That carnal mind led him into sin and keeps him there. His subordination to the carnal mind is the very thing that constitutes him a sinner. The carnal mind makes one man worldly, and another covetous, and another intemperate, and another impure. It makes all of them alike sinful. They have a single mind to indulge appetite and passion as prompted by desire, and in disobedience of reason.

You let one of these sinners become regenerated and immediately he has a double mind. Regeneration implants in him the choice of God as his supreme portion, and gives him a mind, an intention to please and serve him. But regeneration does not remove the "old man," the "carnal mind." All theologies of the world admit this. "Sin," "indwelling sin," " the carnal mind," remains. So the justified Christian has the regenerated mind and "the carnal mind" coexisting in his heart. Paul pictured such a man in vivid language, as if it were himself, in these words: "That which I do I allow not: for what I would that do I not; but what I hate, that do I. It is no more I that do it but sin that dwelleth in me. When I would do good, evil is present within me. I find a law (a uniform tendency) in my members warring against the law of my mind and bringing me into captivity to the law of sin

which is in my members. O wretched man that
I am, who shall deliver me from the body of this
death!"

It is an awful picture; but every Christian of
much experience in the justified life knows its reality. He has himself felt the inner strife and
the contentions of civil war in his own soul. Two
minds,—the one loving, the other hating God.

Now provision has been made for the crucifixion of this "OLD MAN," this "CARNAL MIND." A
cleansing blood has been shed. A sanctifying
Holy Spirit has been given. A Pentecostal blessing is ready. Any Christian who will cast himself on God in utter self-abandonment and full
consecration, and will believe for this blessing
can have it. Holy Ghost fire will burn out the
"carnal mind," and he will know the unutterable
blessing of a pure heart. With purity will come
power and equipment for larger service.

O reader, consent to it; be determined to have
it: pay the price, and the sanctifying Spirit will
fill your heart, and take possession of your life.
"And the peace of God that passeth understanding shall keep your heart and mind through
Christ Jesus." Amen!

SERMON III.

CONSECRATION TO GOD.

Rev. R. L. Selle.

"She of her penury hath cast in all the living that she had." Luke 21:4.

I want to talk to you to-day on the subject of consecration to God, and have selected as a Scripture lesson, Luke 21:1-4, which reads as follows:

"And he looked up, and saw the rich men casting their gifts into the treasury. And he saw also a certain poor widow casting in thither two mites. And he said, Of a truth I say unto you, that this poor widow hath cast in more than they all. For all these have of their abundance cast in unto the offerings of God: but she of her penury hath cast in all the living that she had."

The latter clause of the fourth verse is the text: "She of her penury hath cast in all the living that she had."

The time of the incident from which this lesson is taken was Tuesday of Passover week; the place was the Temple in Jerusalem, and the occasion was that of receiving the offerings, commonly called "taking the collection." The money was not gath-

ered at that time by means of "passing the hat."
A chest or "treasury" was placed on the altar,
the contributors arranged in lines and marched in
front of the altar, each dropping his gift into the
treasury.   On this particular occasion "Jesus sat
over against the treasury," on the platform, and
"he looked up" as the people came down the aisles
to make their offerings to God. He saw the amount
contributed, the amount retained, and understood
the motive back of each gift.   He observed carefully the rich, the poor, the men, the women, the
old, the young as they approached the altar with
their offerings.

"And he saw *also;*" the "also" gives a personal
charm to the narrative and points out and empha-
sizes something   special.   There   was   nothing
strange, nothing out of the ordinary in the "rich"
nor in the "all these" of the lesson, but there was
something strikingly personal in the "also." "And
he saw also a certain poor widow casting in thither
two mites."   The extremes had met; the contrast
was evident, and Jesus said: "Of a truth I say
unto you, that this poor widow hath cast in more
than they all: for all these have of their abundance
cast in unto the offerings of God: but she of her
penury hath cast in all the living that she had."

The rich gave "of their abundance," probably a
tithe of their income for a stated period of time,
feeling no doubt that they were generous and
meeting every requirement of the law touching

financial offerings. How different it was with the
"*also*" *giver* who "cast in all the living that she
had!" Her trembling hand held but little, but
that little was all given to God. Her possessions
were few and meager, but she was not afraid to
trust them entirely in the hand of the Lord. Back
of the gift was a heart full of devotion, rich with
love and strong in faith; her manner was simple
and eloquent with holy fervor. The amounts that
others gave or withheld was nothing to her. She
was worshipping God "in Spirit and in truth,"
"as seeing him who is invisible." It is no wonder that
Jesus "looked up" when that woman approached
the altar.

Here is a lesson on consecration, a lesson for
every Christian who is or wants to be wholly the
Lord's. "Repentance toward God, and faith toward our Lord Jesus Christ" are required of the
sinner when he is brought into a justified state
before God; consecration and faith are required of
the believer when his heart is made pure. The
sinner repents and believes for pardon—the believer consecrates and believes for purity. There
is a wide difference between repentance and consecration; between surrendering to God and presenting (making a present of) the body a living
sacrifice to Him. The subject today deals with the
latter and is beautifully illustrated by the lesson
as follows:

1.   The widow presented her offering to God.

She did not make her offering to the church, to
the rabbi, to the poor, nor to be seen of the rich;
she made her offering to God. She did not make
her offering because the church treasury was emp-
ty, nor because repairs on the temple were needed,
nor because new doors to important mission fields
were opening, nor because she heard an eloquent
and convincing appeal for money; she made her
offering to God because she loved Him with all her
heart and wanted to honor Him with all her sub-
stance.

In making her offering to God the widow recognized the fact that a legal, life-binding and ir-
revocable (without sin) transaction was made.
The two mites were no longer hers but God's;
their ownership had been legally transferred by
mutual consent. That which had been hers was
now the Lord's, in His treasury, in his possession,
ready for his use, anywhere, any time, for any
purpose.

Even so; the literal meaning of the term consecration as applied to the Christian in the sense
of presenting his body a living sacrifice to God
is simply *giving to God,* hands, feet, lips, eyes,
tongue, ears, the whole body; heart, mind, motives,
will, time, talent,influence, all, everything *given to
God* as fully and freely and bindingly as the widow's two mites were given to Him; not a consecration to the church, nor to service, nor a mission,
nor an ism, nor a purpose, but to God; a real,

conscious, living transaction witnessed by angels
and sealed in blood. We are God's, not our own,
in his possession, for his service, anywhere, any
.time, any way; to go or stay, to rejoice or weep,
to be whole or suffer, to be something
or nothing, to live or die, "Thy kingdom come,
thy will be done." That's the way the woman
consecrated her money to God; that's the way we
consecrate ourselves to Him.

2. The widow gave "all the living that she
had." Her offering did not represent a fraction
of her possessions, large or small, but "all the living that she had." The rich gave "of their abundance," a tithe, or more, retaining the remainder
of their possessions for the purpose of using them
according to their own desires.

It is to be feared that the "rich" of the lesson
represent a class of people, probably a large class,
who go through the form of consecration but do
not "present" their bodies, their all, to God. They
are willing to present to Him a portion of their
steps, a segment of their time, a part of their service, a small fraction of their hearts, but not
all; they are willing to give "of their abundance"
of motives, of talents, of words, of actions, retaining the remainder as their own to be used according to their own wills. "All these have of their
abundance cast in unto the offerings of God."
"No man can serve two masters." God cannot
depend upon hands, or feet, or tongue, or time

but partially consecrated to Him, for the reason, when He wants to use them they may be found in the employment of some one else. God cannot be a partner to a divided ownership; he doesn't deal in fractions but units. "Render, therefore, to Cæsar the things that are Cæsar's, and to God the things that are God's." "She of her penury hath cast in all the living that she had."

This, as I understand Bible terms, is Scriptural consecration to God, nothing more, nothing less, and may be expected to produce a Bible experience and yield Bible fruit. When we consecrate ourselves thus to God whether during a revival for the promotion of holiness or not, in a church or under a brush arbor, in the field or in our own home, we will find "suddenly" that the time has "fully come" for the heart to be cleansed from all sin. Having presented our all to God naught remains as our own. We "reckon ourselves dead indeed unto sin." Then in a moment, in the twinkling of an eye, immediately, apparently without effort on our part further than having made the consecration to God, faith grasps the promises of the Word, the blood of Jesus is applied to the heart in cleansing, the Holy Spirit witnesses to the work, and a blessed consciousness of being "every whit made whole," "filled with the Holy Ghost," "sanctified wholly," fills the entire being.

SERMON IV.

A THREE-WORD GOSPEL.

Rev. C. F Wimberly

Matt. 11:28, Luke 24:49, Mark 16:15;—"Come," "Tarry," "Go."

The Gospel of Christ as taught by the multiplicity of sects, some with light, others with more light, and still others with most light, is regarded as vague and complicated, shrouded by a veil of mystery. We hear from every quarter; "Lo here;" "Lo there," *This* or *that*. All that ever came before *us* were blinded hypocrites, or dishonest bigots. Religious conceit abounds, yet it is one of Satan's paradoxical twists.

The student of higher mathematics must often simplify the algebraic propositions which are made up of letters, figures, exponents, and signs—piling up until they resemble Egyptian hieroglyphics. The student of Biblical truth is also overwhelmed by ponderous volumes, prodigious terminologies, bristling with Greek, Latin, Hebrew, and Syriac phrases; written not to lead men to God, and help them to love His truth, but to show forth a great scholarly mind.

The land is gorged with a seminary stamp of

preaching—*words, words, words.* What we need
is not a "Forward movement," but a great *back-
ward* movement, back to the simple gospel, as
taught by Jesus, which the common people heard
gladly.

Christ never sought to teach the multitudes, but
rather shrank from them. He poured His whole
system of truth into a few unsophisticated hearts;
He simplified and focused. Sunbeams never reach
a temperature high enough to burn dry stubble;
but focus them through a convex lens and we can
kindle a fire in zero weather. We desire in this
discourse to simplify the whole Gospel—reduce it
to its lowest terms. A world-wide message in
three words.

I. The first cardinal, fundamental, comprehensive Gospel word is found in Matt. 11:28:
"Come."

1. If we analyze the *why* of all our church ma-
chinery and religious literature—the teaching of
Jesus, the sending the Holy Ghost, the organization of the church, the call of preachers, the cause
of missions ,the founding and endowment of col-
leges, it is all to enlarge, intensify, and make more
efficient Christ's invitation to *come.* We want to
advertise this world-wide invitation to be saved.

2. Let us analyze this great word Come. From
what and to what.

(a)   There must be a coming away from sin.
The separation must be complete. Not a part of

us, but all—God can save no one who refuses to give up all sin. "Leave your sins for the blood to cover," and you will find honey in the rock of salvation.

(b) There must be a coming away from evil associations. "Come out from among them and be ye separate," is as explicit as the coming away from sin.

(c) In coming away from *sin* and *evil associa-* tions, we come away from the bondage of sin and death. The cruel servitude of two worlds is struck off the body and soul. From eternal death to eternal life.

(d) It means a coming to the Throne of mercy; not justice, but mercy. It is coming to a place where we can find help in every time of need.

(e) The invitation of Jesus is to the hungry, of life, to the rest of soul, to the steadfast hope— thirsty, hopeless, foot-sore world to come to the fountain of living water, to the feast of the bread the everlasting anchor.

II. The second cardinal, fundamental, comprehensive Gospel word is found in Luke 24:49, "Tarry." Christ laid special emphasis on this word: "Wait for the promise of the Father," stay in Jerusalem until you are endowed. He would not suffer them to open the world-wide campaign until the promise of Joel be fulfilled.

1. Here is the very core of His plan for the world's evangelization. This His specific com-

mand has been disobeyed. The "Dark Ages" would
never have been, had the *converts* continued to *tarry*. 1900 centuries have passed and yet the world
stumbles and reeks in sin and darkness, because,
we have not obeyed our Lord's command to tarry until the enduement comes from on high. The
church is wearing itself out trying to find a substi-
tute for this needed power. Preachers are threat-
ened, the people brow-beat; we hear the cry of
coveteousness, disloyalty, etc., etc., but what the
whole church needs is to *tarry*.. What are some
of the things being done to supply this needed
power: preachers must know more. More education, more culture; the churches must be more
modern in their work of reaching men, the build-
ings should be equipped, acoustics studied and
mastered; comfort, convenience and entertainment
of the people must be guarded. Our schools must
be endowed, great men from Berlin and Liepsic
should give our young people the best training.
More money must be given for missions. The
doors are open and we must enter.

All this is only secondary. If the church would
go back to this original commandment and *obey*
every need would be supplied.

2. Where must the church tarry? It must be
"upper-room" in character. If show, pretense,
or personal ends be in view, the tarrying will be
fruitless. It must be at an altar of entire consecration. Jesus sent the 120 there to cure them

of ambition, of error concerning Himself, His kingdom, and His work.

3. How long must the church tarry—How long must we tarry? Until entirely emptied of *self*— until the surrender is complete. This part of our preparation was typified by the "burnt offering." The burnt offering all went up—it was consumed. No part was eaten by the priests. The tarrying must be prolonged until we be endued with power from on high—until we receive the Baptism of the Holy Ghost. Whether we seek it for *service* or for *cleansing*, if we stop short of that the tarrying will be incomplete, and the results unsatisfactory. An army without guns, cannon and ammunition could never win a battle. Japan tried to frighten Com. Perry when he sailed into the bay of Yoko- homa by tin-pans and shouts, but they met the stern implements of war and soon surrendered. Oh, the church is wise these days, but it is wise in its own conceit, and not from above. Heavenly, god- ly, Christly wisdom is to *tarry*.

III. The third cardinal, fundamental, compre- hensive Gospel word is found in Mark 16:15: "Go." In this command lies the climax of God's redemptive scheme, and is equally imperative as the "Come" or the "Tarry." Many think it not necessary to go; that it does not apply to all. Jesus said: "Teaching them to observe all things what- soever I have commanded you." The trouble is not that the church does not believe we should

Go; but the real trouble is that the church does not Tarry. It is really easier to Go than to Tarry. Those who Go before they Tarry go in their own strength, and that means without power. For seventeen centuries we have been going without the enduement, hence the miserable failure, the confusion before our enemies.

1. The Come and Tarry are completed in the Go, but if either the first or the second be omitted, Christ's plan of salvation is defeated. The Go without the Tarry has always been a failure, whether it be one eminent in the schools, an ecclesiastical nabob, or a plain circuit rider. Christ's commanding words apply to all regardless of who or what. Let us raise a question: Who is the greatest offender, the man who fails to come, or fails to Tarry or Go? Oh, you say, nothing can be so ruinous as to reject the Gospel invitation; they are without God and without hope—they are lost. Well, if the comers to Christ do not Go, others will be lost. If those who go fail to Tarry their ability to reach the unsaved is largely destroyed, and whose soul is worth most? Christ died for all. What excuse can we give in the great day for such criminal disobedience?

2. Again: Can any man love God and souls, and turn a deaf ear to the Macedonian Cry? Such a faith is *unbiblical, unchristlike,* and *inconsistent.* I dislike the term Foreign Missions. It has done great harm. It gives ignorance, narrow-

ness, and selfishness a chance to look wise and un-load platitudes. When the Holy Ghost is come upon the church—ignorant, narrow, selfish—she at once begins to testify at Jerusalem, Judea, Samaria, and unto the uttermost parts of the earth. There is no authority for a division of our prayers or labors. Those qualified were given work under the Holy Ghost in the regions beyond.

3. Another thing I see under the sun: enthusiasm, leadership and apparent zeal for foreign work and no interest whatever for the lost at our doors. A layman gives $5,000 for Foreign Missions, $1,-000 special for Cuba, and not one cent to support a Door of Hope for the fallen girls within six blocks of his home. Who has not listened to bright, touching papers about the heathen, while throat and ears dazzle with gems sufficient to support a worker for two years—100 times as much spent for tobacco as for the Macedonians—the price of two souls on one finger.

4. Who shall Go? This is answered by asking who shall come? One is co-extensive with the other. The one who comes *only,* is self-centered; God saves no one for himself unless at death, as the dying thief. The one who Comes must Go, or be untrue to a sacred charge.

5. Where shall we go? The wide, wide world —every creature. "The world lieth in sin and darkness." "Jesus is the Light of the world." Where shall we go? To those of our own house-

hold; to those about us. If we do not seek and pray for the nearby ones, our prayers and labors will end with their beginning.

The Go is as wide as the atonement. "Not interested" you say. Nearly 1,000,000,000 unsaved in the regions beyond. 100,000 die daily—each tick of the watch a soul goes out into midnight darkness—10,000 sold into slavery each year. Do you not see the happy villages of Africa raided by Arabs—all who can not travel are killed—babies thrown from the point of bayonets into the grass. 10,000 pure girls sold into lives of shame to pay vows to the gods.

Let us all by the grace of God, *Come* and *Tarry* and *Go*.

SERMON V.

HOLINESS AND THE CHURCH.

Rev. Joseph H. Smith.

"I speak concerning Christ and The Church."
Eph. 5:32.

Let us hear, at the outset, just what it is that
this inspired apostle speaks concerning Christ and
the Church. It sounds very much like a love
story; and presents an analogy from love life.
"Husbands, love your wives, even as Christ also
loved the Church, and gave Himself for it; that
he might sanctify it and cleanse it by the washing
of water through the word, that he might present
it to himself a glorious church not having spot or
wrinkle, or any such thing, but that it should be
holy and without blemish."

This, then, that He speaks concerning Christ
and the Church will form the basis of our re-
marks this morning; that we may have the right
conception of the Church; that we may treasure
our relation to her; that we may recognize the
Church as furnishing the great avenue for holiness work, and our respective relation to her and
to her ministry as most valuable to this end. And
more especially that we may know the sublime re-

lationship into which we are brought with Christ
Himself by reason of our place in His Church, is
the purpose of our message to-day.

Few know it, but it is true that I once came
very near becoming a come-outer. This is the
way it happened. My sensitive soul became pained
and distressed at what corruptions I saw in the
Church, and because of her sectarian divisions,
her self-seeking ministers, her amusements, side-
shows, and questionable means of making money,
etc.   I began to reason that to remain in the
Church amid such conditions compromised my
conscience and that I must "come out" and be
separate.   Fortunately though, I had a friend, a
rich counsellor, deep in piety, versed in the things
of the Spirit, matured in judgment and in love,
"Old John Thompson," we all about Philadel-
phia called him.   He was the young preachers'
friend. I went to him in my distress. Somewhat
to my surprise he agreed much with me. Said
these things were wrong, and they disturbed his
own soul, too. But he had prayed them through
and found that perfect love's plan amended
church conditions that were neither ideal nor
perfect. Then he asked me these two questions:
"Bro. Smith, do you think in these matters the
church is any worse than it was when she had still
strength left to give you birth into the kingdom?"
"No," I promptly said, "No, only I notice it
more." "Well, then again, Brother Smith, do you

remember how she led you into the Canaan of perfect love; and would you cast off whatever might be able to do that for a young convert, as plain as the church weakness is, nowadays, supplemented by so many auxiliary means of promoting holiness?"

Well, that settled come-outism for me. I've never had any trouble on that point since. I prize the Church above all institutions on earth, and will employ all my ministries and all the means of spreading holiness to help rather than hurt the Church my Savior bought with His precious blood.

We must take several views of the Church.

First as a temple. The great divine infinite beauty is not to be all revealed in any one of us as an individual. Not the one, but all are the temples of the living God, and God's dwelling is in the midst of *us*, and the Church viewed in this sense is the incarnation of the Holy Ghost. Just the same as the man Jesus was the incarnated Son. God in the individual was the Christ. God in the body of believers is the church. I look at the church again, and it is called the household of faith; and this is what this epistle beautifully expresses. Don't know that you will find it anywhere else in the Bible, representing the church as a *family*, but here it is more plainly and beautifully put. He says: "The whole family in heaven and earth." The whole family—think of it.

We are not in a different family from those who
have gone before.   We are around the same
friends with Abraham, with John, with Wesley
and with Knox, etc. It is an unbroken family.
Some have gone up to the second story parlor,
while we remain in the basement, but we are in
the one house. It is the family of God.

Jesus is preaching and some one tells Him that
His relations are without wanting to speak with
Him. "His mother and brethren." He says,
"Who is my mother and my brethren. These
are my kinsmen who do the will of my Father.
They are my loved ones." The Church is the
family of God, and we are in that family.

We look at the Church again as the repository
of *inspired truth*. Paul speaks of the Church in
this way. It is the pillar and ground of the
truth. And you and I, if we are members of the
true Church, are stewards of the truth of God.
I look at it again and it is an observatory.
The Church is a watch-tower and an observatory.
From its summit, the watchman sees the stars of
hope and reads the promises of coming glory.
Again the watch-tower of the church is to read
signs of the times, to seal the destiny of nations,
to see from this top view the will of God, and
give a warning unto the heedless and sinful that
are not in the church. A great many are not on
the way to glory, and I have thought sometimes,
beloved, that the watch-towers in our temples were

being neglected. We have a sure word of prophecy.

I look at the Church again as a great
military army. Now brethren and sisters you will
find the places of your destinations. I don't say
we will ever be without denominations; I cannot
tell that. Denominationalism is one thing and
sectarianism is another thing. There are some
houses built with but one room. But these different
denominations are different rooms opening into
the one great court of the Lord. You are right
never to relinquish the spirit of army loyalty. If
you are a Baptist, you ought to be faithful. If you
are a Methodist you ought to be faithful. If you
are a Presbyterian, you ought to be faithful. That
spirit of loyalty to the church is right carried to
a certain stage. College spirit is right, national
spirit is right, and so you and I as we belong to
the different regiments in this great army, want
this spirit; nevertheless, we must rise higher than
our own regiment, for it is not the whole thing.
We may have a proper place for state pride, loyalty and citizenship, but we have a still greater
place for national loyalty to the head of our feder-
al government. Just so with us, we want to be
true to our respective regiments, and ever loyal
to the whole army.

I want to find in a moment the corner stone of
the church, and try and see whether or not you
are in line. But please linger here. The inter-

denominational spirit of holiness, while it means
death to sectarianism, is not death to loyalty. We
are members of different churches, and have the
right to holiness in our different regiments, and
I would never give up that right except by force.
I would purpose as a member of the church to do
my best in the spread of holiness, and use my
church membership and ministerial relations to
their fullest extent for Holiness. So I would
have you treasure the membership of your particular church.

You never hear from this pulpit anything that
would draw you away from your own church obli-
gations. We despise sectarianism on one hand
and come-outism on the other, but we urge you
to be loyal to your own denomination and church,
and there stand for holiness. You hear some people say, our church has more holiness than yours;
come over with us. No, your church has but little
holiness, and if you have any, you had better s'ay
lest they have not any at all. Let your light
shine there. We must not narrow down to that.
Whether Baptist, Methodist or any other church
where we find the need of holiness, we have
a mission with that church in the spread of it,
as well as in the great interdenominational movement alone.

The great thing to know is, whether you are in
the church or not. The possibilities are that some
of you are not. Oh, you may say Bro. Smith,

I belong to this, that or the other church.   But
let me ask you to hold a minute.   I get sick at
heart when I go to great conventions and con-
ferences and hear ministers get up and tell how
many members they have, and so on.

Look here, if some one in your house, or in
your family connection takes the dropsy, would
you go all around town telling people how big
they are getting?   The bigness of many of the
churches is dropsy.   It needs tapping instead of
publicity, and I want you to be very careful how
big yours gets, because it may need a surgical
operation.   I recall a brother, friend of mine.   The
last time I saw him he was at a campmeeting
where he had gone for a rest.   He came under the
influence of holiness preaching, and I remember
well the Sunday morning while I was preaching,
he plunged in and was sanctified wholly.   He was
pastor of a large church.   What was the first
thing do you think he did as a result of his entire sanctification?   He turned out 100 members.
He tells that since that time they have had a
steady stream of God's saving power, and persons
have not only been coming into his church, but
into the true church of the living God.

You will find various efforts put forth, and
ideas advanced that the church is an organization
or institution for society and the like.   The
church is a body.   It is a divine institution and
its mission something higher than reform work.

These are only secondary to the church itself. The church itself does not stand on this, the ban of human institution. The church is built on what? Some one will tell us that it is built on Peter. I was very much amazed on a recent visit to New Orleans when I was carried around in the morning and saw the children kissing the great toe of an image of Peter as an act of worship. It pained my heart to see folks in our own country and even so near us doing this. Beloved, Peter is not the rock upon which the church is built. You will remember the time that Jesus said unto Peter, "Thou art Peter and upon this rock I will build my church." Before the day was over, Jesus had to rebuke Peter as an ally of the devil. It is not Peter. What is the rock? It is important to know what the corner stone of the church is, for from this we will get what constitutes the membership of the church. What did Jesus mean when He said "Upon this rock I will build my church?" It is the experimental knowledge of Christ Jesus. A divine revelation in the heart of Christ as the Savior. That is the rock. The knowledge of Christ as the Messiah revealed to the heart by God Himself. In other words, an experimental knowledge of the Son of God.

I speak here carefully and prayerfully. I want it to be known that one of the reasons the church is in the condition it is in today is, men and women are brought into the church today on another

basis than that of the saving power of the Lord
Jesus Christ.

I have just had occasion to refer to the Bap-
tists. I feel safe about a church that requires a
testimony as to the saving power of Jesus Christ
and not simply the acceptance of a creed. My
brethren and sisters, I don't care how long you
have been in the Baptist, Methodist, or the Presbyterian, or any other church, if you have not been
born again, you are not in the true church; you
are not in the church of the living God.

The spiritual knowledge of Christ as the Son of
God is the corner stone. I want to see the time,
brethren and sisters, when those who administer
the affairs of the church will wake up along this
line, for their own sakes and for the sake of those
coming into their church.

I had a friend,—what a grand man he was.
He was a father to Illinois Methodism. He came
to the church at one time that was badly split and
torn. There was one element that would not work
with another element. He dealt with them pa-
tiently, and first went to see them personally and
tried to bring them together, but there was no
revival.

He astonished the congregation one morning
by saying, I am going to open the doors of the
church. They knew no one had been converted,
no professions, and it had only been customary to
open the doors of the church when someone had

been converted. He said to them, "It is going to be the back door, and I want the following members to come forth." He called forward several officials and their wives, and a few who were not officers. With tears streaming down his cheeks he said to them: "You have become a curse to the church; you have hindered God's work, and you have been in the way of the salvation of souls for several ministries. I have dealt with you personally, I have visited your homes and tried to bring about a revival. Now without causing the church any further disturbance, I want you, as you gave your hand years ago to the pastor to join, I want you to take my hand and withdraw." Men and women withdrew, realizing that they were without the church of God. The result was a great revival season. The community was moved, hearts were stirred and for weeks the revival went on, and before the weeks had closed, most of those who had withdrawn, had been converted and brought back into the church again.

Brethren and sisters, I fear that the church in many places has gotten on a wrong footing. The eagerness for members and the desire for social position have been so great that they have shifted away from the real church foundation. All those who are in the church on any other basis other than that of experimental religion, are not in the church at all. They are in a shed adjoining the church. Only those who know Christ as their

Savior are in the real church. Now, friends, don't be in a hurry to get them out of the shed. Have an altar, try to get them converted and brought into the true church of the living God.

I speak concerning Christ and the church, the church without spot or blemish.

In a distant city, working in a manufacturing establishment, was a young woman. A beautiful girl she was. She was of good parentage but very poor, and with no education. She acquired the painting art in connection with the business there, and was very successful too. She being a very popular young lady, the head of the firm rested his eye upon her and fell in love with her. The head of the concern in love with a girl in his mill who could neither read nor write? He made provisions by which she was educated. First, by a tutor; later she was placed in an academy, and later in college, and after college days were over, she came back a polished young woman to be his bride, to be the wife of his life, the queen of his home, and to share his fortunes and comforts. I saw her in her home and she told me this story, and said, "I am now helping him pour out his money for God and for souls."

The church of God, what has it been taken from? What ignorance! Jesus saw it when it was no church at all, when it was only a possibility, only a germ, and He loved it. Christ fell in love with the church. Have you ever wondered why

Christ never married. He came to share all human experiences that He might sympathize and save, yet He never married. It was not that He disapproved of marrying. He honored a marriage ceremony with His first miracle. Was Christ never a lover? Was he only divine in His life? Had He no human love? I will tell you why He never married. There was a blending in Christ's heart of the human and the divine, and there was no one person to be found that could be the object of the Savior's heart. So He reserved His love for the whole church. The whole church is the bride of Christ. He loves the whole church like a husband loves his wife. When a natural love springs up in your heart, as it will, and the desire for companionship, let me remind you that Christ also loved, and you need not fear to bring this to Jesus. You need not fear to bring your heart affections to the Lord.

Christ loved the church. He took her when she was in ignorance as did the man the young woman. He took her when she could neither read nor write, into his society. She would have had a life long embarrassment, had he not in His wisdom made provision by which she could be fitted and prepared to be His wife. They were never embarrassed or ashamed.

Now mark, I have not said that the grace of entire sanctification is the corner stone on which the church is built. That is a mistake when peo-

ple say that.   There are those in the church who
have only been justified, and rightly they belong
there.   Little folks are what we make grown up
folks out of.   So we have been careful not to say
that the grace of entire sanctification is the corner
stone of the church.   Men are justified before they
are sanctified, and you have a right to go into
the church as soon as you are regenerated.

Look at the church in that state; Christ could
have transferred the church to heaven, but what
an embarrassment without cleanness of heart, and
Christ would have been eternally embarrassed to
have brought before the angels, and in the presence of the Father, His bride.   I have good news
for you.   In the centuries and millenniums to
come, Christ is never going to apologize for you.
He is never going to apologize because He has
made you His bride.   He loved the church and
gave Himself for it that He might sanctify it
through His blood, that He might present it to
Himself a Holy Church without spot or blemish.

I seem to hear wedding bells, there is a mighty
thundering, a great roaring of the seas.   I seem
to hear the sound of a great chorus, and they are
all saying, "Hallelujah, hallelujah, hallelujah,
the marriage of the Lamb is come and His bride
has made herself ready."   There is a great big
wedding day ahead of us.   The Son of God is
going to be married.   Have you the invitation?
No, you are the bride.   You will be in the glory

of the Son of God. Don't you see what a large
place the ministry to the church should occupy?
God doesn't do these things without agencies or
without ministry. There is a great dearth in
most of our ministerings, and most of our churches, because there is so little being ministered directly for the sanctification of the church, but God
has put upon some of us that we will minister full
salvation unto every true member of the church
in order that we may be ready for the wedding of
the Lamb. Yes, this is a glorious church: There
are many things I would like to say about the
church.

My brethren and sisters, I would never be satisfied if I were out of the church. If you are
in the church, make sure that you have a right
to be there. I would not be in a hurry to get
out. If you find that you do not know Christ as
your personal Savior, I would suspend all active
church duties, but I would not withdraw. I would
suspend teaching the Sunday school class should
you be a teacher. I would not make another turn
to do anything in the church until I got right
with God. Get on the wedding garment He has
provided. Then you can be a member of Methodist, Baptist or any other church, as these are only
nicknames. I would be a member of the real
church without spot or blemish. Let us never
be seeking to divide the church. Never be seeking
to put people out.

SERMON VI.

THE LIGHT OF THE WORLD.

Rev. E. P. Ellyson.

"As long as I am in the world, I am the light of the world." John 9:5. "Ye are the light of the world." Matt. 5:14.

1. *Jesus is the Light of the World.*

In our first text Jesus plainly declares Himself to be the Light of the World. It seems very strange that any right-minded person should for a moment question the truth of this declaration, especially a person living in an enlightened country. Who can read the history of the world and not see Christ as the Light of the World? A partial idea of what the world would be without Christ may be seen by a glance at the heathen who do not now have the gospel. Truly this would be a dark world if it were not for Jesus.

But the text seems to imply that this light is only for a time. "As long as I am in the world" might seem to indicate that Christ is the Light of the world only so long as He is in the world, and that He will sometime leave the world. And there is a sense in which this is true, and in an-

other it is not true. Notice that it does not say,
"As long as I am in the world in the flesh I am
the Light of the world." Being in the world to-
day in His spiritual presence He may, so far as
the text is concerned, be the Light of the world.
But the statement of the text seems to have some
special reference to His presence in the world in
the flesh. Let us see how this is. Following His
ascension, if He is still the Light of the world
there must be a change in the manifestation of
that light. He is now no longer the Light in the
sense of His personal bodily presence in the
world. There is then a sense in which He ceases
to be the Light of the world. But the Light still
shines, and shines in connection with a personal
bodily presence.

2. *The Church is the Light of the World.*

Our second text is the statement of Jesus to
His disciples, informing them that they are the
light of the world. These disciples are the nu-
cleus of the Church. That the Church is the light
of the world ought no more to be questioned than
that Christ is the Light of the world. Taking the
two texts together we are told that so long as Jesus
is in the world He is the Light of the world, but
now that He has gone out of the world the church
is the light of the world. Who would want to
live in the world to-day if there were no churches
in the world? Just think of the condition of the
towns and communities where they have no

churches. Not one of us would want to live there, and bring up our children in such a place. Surely the Church is the light of the world.

3. *The Church's Light is but Reflected Light.*

Now that we have seen that Christ is the Light of the world, and that the Church is the light of the world we ask, are there two lights, and does the church supersede Jesus as the Light of the world? We answer, No, there is but one true light. Jesus is the Light of the world, and the Church is the light of the world only as it is the reflector of Jesus the Light. Let us see if the Bible will not bear us out in this statement. We will have to confine ourselves to two simple illustrations, one of which we will give very briefly, and the other more extendedly.

4. *The Golden Candlesticks.*

In the first chapter of Revelation John gives us the account of his first vision. In this vision he sees one, who evidently is Jesus Christ, walking in the midst of seven golden candlesticks. In the last verse the figure of the candlesticks is interpreted. "The seven candlesticks which thou sawest are seven churches." The candlestick is not a light and can not shine, but it is a light-holder and can hold the light up where it will shine. The Church, then, is not a source of light, but is simply a light bearer to hold up the true light. The true light is Christ, and Christ in the Church, the candlestick, is the light of the world. By His presence in the Church He makes it the light of the world. This is our first illustration.

5. *Two Great Lights.*

For our second illustration we will turn to the account of the creation of lights in the first chapter of Genesis. "And God said, "Let there be lights in the firmament of heaven to divide the day from the night; and let them be for signs, and for seasons, and for days and years; and let them be for lights in the firmament of heaven to give light upon the earth; and it was so. And God made the two great lights; the greater light to rule the day, and the lesser light to rule the night." Here we have two great lights and their five fold object. They are for (1) light upon the earth, (2) to divide the day and night, (3) to mark the seasons, (4) to mark the year, and (5) for signs. All are familiar with how these lights are for days, seasons, and years, but how are they signs? They have been used many times as signs during the past, and prophecy informs us that they will continue to be so used. For example, "The sun shall be turned into darkness, and the moon into blood, before the day of the Lord come," and at the crucifixion "a darkness came over the whole land until the ninth hour, the sun's light failing." But these great lights are signs in still another sense. In Mal. 4:2, the coming of Jesus is spoken of as the rising of the "Sun of Righteousness." Notice that it is sun and not son.

The sun as the light of the world is a picture or
figure of Jesus as the Light of the world. The
sun is a sign-type of Jesus. But what of the
Church as the light of the world? From Joseph's
dream and its interpretation we may discover the
figurative interpretation of the moon. Joseph
dreamed that the sun, moon, and the eleven stars
did him obeisance. His father, by the aid of the
Spirit, interpreted the dream by saying, "Shall
I and thy mother, and thy brethren indeed come
to bow down ourselves to thee to the earth." Gen.
37:10. By this interpretation the sun stands for
the husband, the moon for the wife, and the stars
for the children. Jesus then is the husband, and
the moon must stand for His bride or wife. By
turning to Eph. 5:25, where it says, "Husbands
love your wives even as Christ also loved the
Church," and the accompanying verses, we will
see that the Church is Christ's bride or wife. The
figure of the Church as the Light of the world.
The moon is a sign-type of the Church.

We are all familiar with the fact of the source
of the moon's light. The sun by day and the
moon by night are both the light of the world.
But after all there is but one light, for the moon
is but the reflection of the light from the sun
which has now gone down. And is not this the
Church's position in the world, reflecting the light
and glory from the hidden Christ. The moon is but
a cold, dead mass and utterly powerless as a light

except the light from the sun shines upon it.   So
the Church, though it may have the best of methods, a most magnificent building, an eloquent
preacher, a superior choir, and a large, intelligent
membership, will be dead, cold, and formal, and
will be useless in the world except the light from
Jesus shines upon it.   Behold in this the reason
for the Church's lack of power in these days.

6. *When They Shine.*

The sun and the moon are for light upon the
earth and as lights are still further signs of Christ
and the Church.   Our reading in Genesis told us
that the sun is for the day and the moon is for the
night.   What a blessing to the world that when
the sun disapppears the moon appears to give
light upon the earth.   How very dark is the night
when the moon does not shine.   But this is no
more true of the sun and moon than of Christ and
the Church.   Christ is to rule earth's day and
the Church earth's night.   Nearly two thousand
years ago the "Sun of Righteousness" arose over
Judea's hills and began to shine from Bethlehem's manger.   But this was only the beginning
of a very short day.   In thirty-three brief years we
see this Sun setting, and earth's night again beginning.   On Calvary's cross He hung low on the
horizon, and for three hours the natural sun hid
his face and refused to give his light, thus pic-
turing the darkness of the earth without this light
of the world, now going down.   But scarcely had

this "Sun of righteousness" fully set behind the western cloud banks until, by the coming of the Holy Spirit on the day of Pentecost, the Church was formed and thus the moon arose to rule the night. Yes, this is still earth's night, dark with the presence of sin. Oh, what a blessing this coming up of the Church as the custodian of light, glorious gospel light and life. Let us every time we are out on a moonlit night and look up and see the beautiful moon just stop long enough to thank God for the glorious Church of which the moon is such a beautiful type. Let us magnify the Church in this her work of reflecting the glory of the hidden Christ in this part of earth's night in which we are living.

The Church is made up of individuals and the brightness of her light depends somewhat, at least, upon the brightness of the shining of each individual. The Church bearing the relation to the spiritual world which the moon does to the natural world, brings great responsibility upon both the Church and the individual. Just think of it! Christ, the Light, is gone, is hidden from the view of the natural eye, and now He shines upon the world through saved men and women. What if we should refuse to shine; how very dark the night would be. We need to feel more largely our individual responsibility. We are not saved simply to have a good time and enjoy ourselves, we must shine. Jesus speaking to the Father concerning the disciples said, "As thou hast sent me into the world, even so have I also sent them into the world," and He commanded them, "Let your light so shine before men, that they may see your good works and glorify your Father which is in heaven." The Lord help us to shine brightly and reflect the light of Christ in the darkness about us. I do pray that none may lose their way in this night of sin because of any lack of mine or yours in shining.

7. *What Hinders the Shining.*

The sun always shines. Something may intercept its rays so that they can not reach certain objects but nothing can stop it from shining. But the moon sometimes does not shine at all. When is it then that the moon does not shine? At the same time let us ask, what it is that keeps the moon from shining as brightly some times as it does at other times? A little careful thought just here will show us that the moon always shines brightly except when the earth or something pertaining thereto gets between it and the sun. If the earth gets between the moon and the sun, then we have an eclipse, either partial or total. If a cloud, which is something pertaining to the earth, gets between the moon and the sun, then the light is dimed to a greater or less extent. It is just so with the Church. It is worldliness that hinders the shining of the Church. The Church's light has been greatly dimmed by her worldly spirit and worldly methods, and some special churches have even gone into a total eclipse. Worldliness will ruin any church. The world in this, her night, needs the brightest light she can get. It is a great sin for the Church to allow her light to be dimmed. Every door of the church should be tightly barred against worldliness. But alas! how wide open they have been. Behold again the secret of the Church's lack of power and influence in the world to-day. Oh that everywhere she would get out from behind these clouds of worldliness where the full rays from the "Sun of Righteousness" can strike her directly, and reflect from her brightly upon the earth.

Holiness is the experience the Church must have if she accomplishes this result, if she fulfills this her great mission to the world. Without holiness there will be clouds to hinder the brightness of the shining. It is holiness in the Church that makes it a clean and polished reflector of the divine glory. We are familiar with the statement that without holiness no man shall see the Lord, and believe that holiness is essential for one to come into the personal presence of God and look into His face. But this truth goes farther. Only as a man is holy can another person see God in him, and in proportion to the intensity of that holiness will be the brightness of the light. Holiness is the need of the day, and we need to go on perfecting holiness in the fear of the Lord. While they may not be loved by the worldly membership in the Church yet the holy people are the true light in the Church. It is the holy people that largely make the Church the light of the world, for it is they who are in the condition to brightly reflect the light of Christ. It is the holy people that know of unclouded communion with Christ, that produce revivals, that see the display of God's power. The Lord grant us more holiness in the world, in the Church.

8. *The Sun to Again Come Up.*

Yes, we are praising the Lord for the glorious Church. But as glorious as is the present position of the Church in the world its glory is soon to be out done by the greater glory of the rising of the "Sun of Righteousness." The present period of earth's night is not to continue forever. It must give way for the glorious millennial day when Jesus comes again to rule the world. That the "Sun of Righteousness" will again arise, or that Jesus will come again can not well be doubted by any Bible reader. The angels so definitely announced that "this same Jesus, which is taken up from you into heaven, shall so come in like manner as ye have seen Him go into heaven," that to doubt the literal second coming of Christ is to call in question the veracity of the angels or the Bible. And surely the second coming of the Lord will usher in a glorious day, for then Satan will be bound and shut up in the bottomless pit, the

kingdoms of this world will become the kingdom of Christ; holiness will prevail and righteousness will cover the earth as the waters cover the
sea. Then will the lion and ox lie down together
and every man may sit under his own, yes his
own vine or fig tree, and nothing will hurt nor
harm him. The thorn will give way to the fir
tree and the earth bring forth in richness. Truly
this will be a glorious day when both the sun and
the moon will shine together, for Christ will reign
with His bride. Shall we not do all in our power
to hasten that glorious day

SERMON VII.

THE MIND OF THE MASTER.

Rev. Will H. Huff.

"But we have the mind of Christ." 1 Cor. 2:16. "Let this mind be in you which was also in Christ Jesus." Phil. 2:5.

In Paul's letter to the Corinthians, he said, "We have the mind of Christ;" in his message to the Philippians, he said, "Let this mind be in you." We have in this two-fold statement of truth a positive declaration and a striking injunction. It is the statement of an essential fact in salvation and the injunction to realize it in experience. Throughout the Pauline epistles he was solicitous that the church possess in experience what was provided in redemption. Writers tell us that the word "mind" in the first passage is not identical with that of the second. The first has to do more with that spiritual intelligence or consciousness in its relation to divine things. The second has to do more with the characteristics of the mind of the Master as He came in touch with men.

It is my purpose in this message to deal with the mind of Christ as to its spiritual consciousness; the mind of Christ as to its characteristics; the mind of Christ as to the how of our fullest possession of it.

1. *The declaration*—"*We have the mind of Christ.*"

In dealing with Christian consciousness Paul suggests the possibility of three conditions. He speaks of the "natural man, who receiveth not the things of the Spirit of God; for they are foolishness unto him; neither can he know them, for they are spiritually discerned." He further declares that in this natural condition man's understanding is darkened, that he is alienated from the life of God and that he has a heart-blindness. Nothing could be more pathetic than to see humanity ignorant of God, unlike God, no appreciation of God, to whom spiritual things are foolishness. Man alive physically, socially, financially and dead spiritually. Humanity dead to deity, spends its days dealing in dust. The sinner in his natural condition can have no Christian consciousness, for Christian consciousness is vitally related to Christian experience and Christian experience is vitally related to Christ.

Again he speaks of the man who is "yet carnal." He says this man is a babe in Christ, has spiritual life, some appreciation of divine things, but is hindered by something he calls carnality. This is a sort of double-minded fellow hindered in his spiritual going, hampered in his spiritual liberty and mixed in his Christian experience. Multitudes have started well but are dwarfed to-day because they have failed to go on to the fullness of the blessing.

Again, he speaks of "he that is spiritual." He says this man discerneth spiritual things, has the mind of Christ, is among them who are perfect and to such an one he can speak wisdom. I think Paul's terms here, "he that is spiritual," "they who are perfect," and "we who have the mind of Christ," refer to those who have been born again out of the natural state, cleansed from the carnal principle and in whose life the restoration of the lost order is restored. This man has a God-consciousness that is not speculation, neither is it reached by logical argument, but is revealed to the spiritually minded by the Holy Ghost.

With this spiritual intelligence we know God, the essential facts of our nature have found a fitting field of operation and we have been brought into the true environment of our life. We have confidence in God and delight in His will. We walk in His light and are unafraid in His presence. We have fellowship with God through life's pilgrimage;we have communion with God through life's plans and pleasures; we have co-operation with God through life's service and activities. We will have a home in the city that hath foundation. And all this is ours because we have the mind of Christ, the intelligence of Christ, the conscious-

ness of Christ, the life of Christ. No wonder
Paul was emphatic in his declaration when he had
in mind this central fact of Christianity, which
was purchased for us in a plenteous redemption.

II. *The injunction—"Let this mind be in you."*

Here, I suppose, we have one of the highest in-
junctions ever given to the people of God. We are
not only to possess the mind of Christ in its spiritual appreciation of divine things, but we are also
to manifest the mind of Christ as we come in contact with men. Of course there are many who
would make themselves busy in telling us that
this would be impossible. They tell us as long as
we live here in a world of sin that we cannot walk
as He walked, love as He loved and represent Him
here among men, but where unbelief would dis-
courage, the Word of God would encourage, and
what would be impossible with a worldling is possible with the genuinely spiritual.

Of course Paul did not mean we were to manifest the mind of Christ in all of its scope of wisdom, greatness and power. He was infinite, we are
finite. He was unlimited, we are limited. He
was all-wise, we are ignorant. He never made a
mistake, we have made serious ones. He never
took a step in the wrong direction, we walked for
years in the wrong way. So it does not mean we
are to possess the mind of Christ in quantity but
in quality. We could take a pitcher, go to the
Atlantic Ocean and fill the pitcher out of the

ocean—we did not get the whole body of water in
the vessel but we got the same kind. We can bring
our small earthen vessel to the great ocean of
divinity and there be filled in our limited capacity
with that which fills the Infinite. John says
"of His fulness have all we received and grace
for grace." He means by this that every grace
that grew, blossomed and bore fruit in the life
of our Lord that we can possess a like grace.

III. *Some of the characteristics* of the mind
of Christ, as they were manifest in the land of
His ministry.

As we notice these characteristics of the mind
of the Master we will ask the Spirit to apply the
truth to our hearts and see if we be like-minded.

1. Humility.

He was the humble-minded Christ.
If we ever have an appreciation of the
significance of our Lord's humiliation we must
get a firm grasp of Paul's splendid passage to the
Philippians. We will take the verses that deal
immediately with this great fact. "Who, being
in the form of God, thought it not robbery to be
equal with God, but made Himself of no reputa-
tion and took upon Him the form of a servant,
and was made in the likeness of men; and being
found in fashion as a man, He humbled Himself,
and became obedient unto death, even the death
of the cross." Here we have Paul's conception
of our Lord's humiliation. He takes us back

through the eternities to the pre-existent Christ. There he declares that Christ was in the "form of God," but in the presence of the call for earth's redemption, He took on Him the *form* of a servant, that is, He came to the level of those needing succor. Thus we have the stoop of divinity on earth's redemptive mission. He passed from Sovereign to servant; for the redemption of men He came from glory to Galilee. He not only took on Him the form of a servant, but also "humbled Himself and became obedient unto death, even the death of the cross." So humility was the secret of our blood redemption. Humility was the warp and woof of the life of our Lord. Humility was the central thought of His teaching. If I am to possess and manifest the mind of Christ, then I must be humble before God, sincere and Christlike in my dealings with men. There is certainly no place for self-importance or self-seeking here, but a large place for the compassion of Christ in the service for humanity.

2. Purity.

He was the pure mided Christ. He said, "which one of you convinceth me of sin?" He said, "The Prince of this world cometh and hath nothing in me." He was prophetically described as "the Lily of the Valley." They are snow-white. His thoughts were pure, His motives were pure, His desires were pure, His propensities were pure, His words were pure. His life was transparent, there was nothing streaked in His nature. He neither talked smut nor listened to smut. If we are to be Christ-minded, then we will go forth among men, as the light of the world, the salt of the earth, and be a living rebuke to the veneered devilishness of the twentieth century.

3.   Patience.

He was the patient Christ. He was patient with His friends and patient with His enemies. His friends were always misunderstanding Him and His enemies were always trying to trap Him. He held onto Simon Peter and said, "I have prayed for thee." He never gave Judas up till Judas said, "How much will you give me for Him?" He never went to pieces under provocation and nothing explosive was found in His nature even under fire. You have met that fellow who says, "Of course I get impatient, of course I get mad, but I am all over it in a minute." Well, the San Francisco earthquake was all over it in a minute, but it left things in such a bad shape that a few more like it would put the real-estate men out of business in that coast town. It is not the awful out-broken sins nor the vicious, vulgar things that are spoiling so many Christians, but those little momentary heart-breaks with God. If we are possessed with the Christ-mind, then patience will have its perfect work and we will rank among those "who are perfect and entire, wanting nothing."

4. Love.

He was the Christ of love. Back of His humility, back of His purity, back of His patience, was the great love-life. Love was the impulse of His service, sorrow and suffering. He had compassion on the multitudes, wept over the city, sought the lost sheep, prayed for His murderers and rescued the dying thief from the jaws of unfolding damnation. "Having loved His own He loved them unto the end." The old word of the decalogue is, "Thou shalt love the Lord thy God." Christ was love revealed. Paul compares love with everything else and gives us its value. He analyses it and gives us its nature. He breaks it up into its component parts and tells us its duration. John says, "As He is, so are we in this world." That is, as He is in His essential nature, so are we in our essential nature, if we have the mind of Christ. The Apostle John uses tremendous language when he describes this love in operation. He says, "If any man *love* the *world, the love of the Father is not in him."* "But whoso hath this world's goods and seeth his brother hath need, and shutteth up the bowels of his compassion from him, how *dwelleth the love of God in him."* If any man say, *I love God, and hateth his brother, he is a liar."* This characteristic of the mind of Christ

delivers us from the world, saves us from stingi-
ness and enables us to love the rest of the family.

5. Unselfishness.

He was the unselfish Christ. He said, "I came
not to be ministered unto, but to minister." There
is nothing more subtle than selfishness. No difference how pure our motive may be at the beginning, if we are not careful and prayerful they
will become mixed. This poisonous element is
manifest in self-will, in that it wants its own way
and plans. It is manifest in self-indulgence, self-
complacency, self-glorying, self-confidence, self-
consciousnesss, self-importance, and self-seeking.
There is no service so sacred, no calling so high,
no precinct so holy but what it will contaminate
if we are not possessed with the mind of Jesus
Christ.

6. Joy.

Christ had a joyful mind. I know the Bible
says that "He was a man of sorrows and acquaint-
ed with grief," that "His visage was marred," and
that "He gave His back to the smiters," but it
also says that Jesus rejoiced in spirit. His joy
broke out under the most unlikely circumstances,
as if it was not dependent on outer signs but of an
inner condition. This joy is the legacy He be-
queathed to His followers. If His mind is ours,
then His joy will be our strength.

7. Aggressiveness.

He was the aggressive Christ. At the begin-

ning of His life He said, "I must be about my
Father's business." At the close of His life He
said, "I have finished the work thou gavest me to
do." Between those two statements He lived a
life of unceasing service for those who were even
unappreciative. For us to be Christ-minded, it
means that we have a blood-earnestness in service
and a zeal of the Lord for work in His kingdom.

8. Loyalty.

He was the loyal-minded Christ. He never
swerved an inch from truth or duty. He was loyal
to God when He was popular, He was loyal
to truth when it cost Him His following. That
was a close sermon He preached that day when
He said, "Except ye eat my flesh and drink my
blood, ye have no part with me." His disciples
said "That is a hard saying; who can hear it?"
They left the meeting, withdrew from the society
and followed Him no more, but as they departed
He did not run after them and apologize for the
truth. There was a handful left. He turned to
Simon Peter and said, "Will ye go away also?"
Peter looked at the crowd going over the hill,
then into the eye of Christ, and said, "Lord, to
whom shall we go? Thou hast the words of eternal life." If we have the mind of Christ, we will
be loyal to truth, loyal to God, loyal to holiness,
even if some camp-followers do leave.

9. Victory.

He was the victorious Christ. For awhile it

looked as if He were a failure. When His own
disciple sold Him for thirty pieces of silver, when
He was arrested in the olive grove, when He stood
in the presence of Pontius Pilate, when He stag-
gered down the streets of Jerusalem and strug-
gled up the hill, when they stripped Him of His
raiment, when we listen to the sickening thud of
the hammer, when we see Him hanging between
two thieves,—it seemed as if He had failed. Hell
thought He was defeated and was jubilant, but it
had been declared through the prophet of old,
"He shall not fail." So amid the reeling earth
and darkening sun and opening graves, there was
a cry, "It is finished." The world was redeemed
and hell was defeated. Figuratively speaking,
there was a rattling at the gates of perdition, the
gates were twisted from their rusty hinges, and
the triumphant One walked through the ashes of
damnation to the throne of darkness and there
pulled the Prince from his throne and threw him
in the ashes and with one foot on his neck, said,
"I am He that liveth and was dead and am alive
forevermore, and have the keys of hell and death
and I open and no man shuts, and I shut and no
man opens." Then after the forty days of the
resurrection, "He ascended above principality and
power and might and dominion and every name
that is named and sat down at the right hand of
the Majesty on high, waiting till His enemies
became His footstool." Victor over sin, flesh, hell

and the grave. If we possess His mind we will be victorious in life, triumphant in death and outshine the sun in the kingdom of our Father.

IV. *The method of obtainment.*

How may I be possessed with the mind of Christ and how may I manifest it among men. There is just one little word in the text that gives us the key. That little word is, *"Let."* This brings us to the point of personal responsibility. The whole message culminates here for the individual. The word "let" suggests abandonment. If we ever come into the possession of this grace, there must be a whole-hearted, absolute, positive, final abandonment to God to be cleansed from sin, made holy in heart and filled with the Holy Ghost. When God speaks the second time, "Be clean," we are then conditioned to be possessed with the mind that was in Christ Jesus.

This ,as a theory, seems easy, but to put it into actual practice is difficult, but there is a hope for every struggling, hungry, discouraged life. Put the past with its failures under the blood, put the future in God's hands, cease your doubting, abide in the will and word of God and *let* Him have His way with thee.

> "Just now your doubtings give o'er,
> Just now reject Him no more,
> Just now throw open the door,
> 　　*Let* Jesus come into your heart."

SERMON VIII.

PERFECT LOVE.

Rev. Clement C. Cary.

"There is no fear in love, but perfect love casteth out fear; because fear hath torment. He that feareth is not made perfect in love." 1 John 4:18.

I. In the text, John does not say that one may not love God and at the same time have some measure of the "fear which hath torment." "There is no fear *in love itself*," nor in a heart completely possessed with love, but there may be those who love God truly and sincerely who have some of the "fear which hath torment."

He does not say, "He that feareth" does not love at all. This would be to contradict religious experience in all ages. But this is what he says: "He that feareth is *not made perfect in love*," plainly indicating there are degrees in love. Love in the heart is the evidence of regeneration. Fear in the heart with love, is the evidence that some of the "remains of the carnal mind" still exist. It simply proves one is not yet made perfect in love—nothing more. Perfect love in the heart casting out all fear is the mark of entire sanctification.

"Fear that hath torment" is not necessarily proof of an unregenerate state. Far from it. It only proves the heart has not been fully delivered from that which gives rise to this fear. Let him who has ears to hear, heed this important truth. Many a converted person suffers from the presence of the fear referred to in the text. To say that these are unregenerate, because of the existence of that fear, will be to grieve those whom God has not grieved, and cause them needlessly to write bitter things against themselves. It will be to give the great "accuser of the brethren" an undue advantage over these weak disciples, who say,

"I hold thee with a trembling hand,
But will not let thee go."

He who would shut these out of the kingdom of grace displays wonderful ignorance of religious experience, and knows precious little of the work of grace in the human heart.

Let no true believer, who consciously loves and obeys God, for one moment doubt his conversion because he is harassed with this tormenting fear. His trouble is not in the spuriousness of his conversion, but rather in the lack of perfect love which casteth out fear. Let him not conclude he is therefore a sinner or a backslider. This is the logic of Satan, who falsely accuses the brethren. Sinners and backsliders do not love God. They cannot love Him till they are either changed or restored. But this believer, though he "feareth," sensibly loves God, and walks obediently before Him. Let him not listen to those who would put him in the unconverted column. Let him rather listen to the voice which says, "Let us go on unto perfection."

2. Here we have proof of the doctrine of "sin in believers." Whence comes this "fear which hath torment," found in converted believers? for there is no question it is found there. To dispute it is to show great ignorance of this first work of grace. This "fear" is not of grace, but is of nature. It belongs to the carnal mind. Its root is sin. Its original source is depravity. It belongs to the "remains of the carnal mind." Its very presence is indicative of something wrong in the heart, something disturbing in its nature, which does not belong to grace. It is closely related to unbelief, in fact it is but the natural offspring of unbelief. It is of the nature of doubt, since a perfect faith is directly opposed to fear, doubt and unbelief.

Now if the "fear which hath torment" is a part of inherited depravity—if it is of the nature of sin—if it be found in converted hearts—then it follows there is "sin in believers."

II. What is perfect love? And what does it do?

1. Perfect love is the pure love of God so filling the heart as to exclude therefrom all unholy tempers, evil desires, wicked dispositions, and sin-

ful tendencies. Love fills the heart, while all that is opposed to love and which is out of harmony with God is excluded. Carnality now has no place therein. It means sincerity, a single eye, pure motives, without the semblance of impurity, insincerity, or mixed motives. It is called "perfect love" simply because Divine love perfectly fills the soul. Everything of the nature of hatred, envy, pride, foolishness, covetousness, jealousy, and evil speakings is ruled out. Love casts out these things. Being entirely filled with love, of course the heart has been entirely emptied of all that is sinful. Love unmixed, unalloyed, unadulterated, possesses and rules the entire spirit of the man. All love is added, all evil is subtracted. Just as a vessel filled allows no room for anything else in it, so the heart filled with pure love permits nothing to remain therein evil in nature or out of harmony with the God of love.

Here is Christian Perfection, the only kind taught in God's Word, the only sort we advocate, and the only kind about which we know anything. It is *perfection in love*—nothing more, nothing less. This is all we claim for it. What objection has any honest man, hunting for the truth, to it? It is a perfect heart, perfect love to God, and perfect love to man. This is what is involved in this precious doctrine.

Hold your mind down to this one thought, and steady yourself, and you cannot go very far astray

on this vital truth. If you fight Christian Perfection, be it understood you oppose perfect love.
If you reject this experience, then you turn from
a heart made perfect in love to God and man.

> "A rest where all our soul's desire
>   Is fixed on things above;
> Where fear and sin and grief expire,
>   Cast out by perfect love."

2.   Perfect love means that state of heart where
the two great commandments laid down by our
Lord are fully obeyed: "Thou shalt love the Lord
thy God with all thy heart," and "Thou shalt
love thy neighbor as thyself."   For only as the
heart is perfected in love by grace divine can these
two things be done. This higher grace places one
where there is supreme love to God and universal
love to man.   It means moral ability imparted
by the Holy Spirit to cheerfully keep these two
great commandments. He then who loves God
consciously with all his heart, and who loves his
neighbor as himself, fulfills God's commands, and
is made perfect in love, for "love is the fulfilling
of the law."

Is this possible? Why not? He who formed
man's heart as a temple in which to dwell Himself, can He not so cleanse and prepare it, as to
exclude everything which is in conflict with the
law of love, and fill it with everything which is

in harmony with Himself, the God of love?

A true husband loves the wife of his bosom with all his heart. He loves her as he loves no other woman, and he loves her above all other women. None but his wife has a place in his affections. This is what law, custom and propriety demand, and nothing else will satisfy public opinion. In this respect, he is a perfect husband. His heart is perfect in love toward his wife. Is that expecting too much of a husband?

Can it not be possible to love God in the same measure, to love Him above all others, and to love Him as we love no one else? Why not? Shall we be able to love with a conjugal love perfectly, and in a greater degree than we can love God with a spiritual love, with the aid of the Divine Spirit? Surely not. Can nature do more for us in loving than can grace? Shall we always sing, "Prone to leave the God I love?"

A sinner loves sin with all his heart, loves sin perfectly, loves sin as he loves nothing else, loves sin above everything else. He is a perfect sinner, his heart is perfect in love toward sin. Sin so possesses him that all holiness is excluded from his heart. Sin dominates him entirely.

Why cannot grace so sanctify the nature that the believer may be in like manner and degree perfect in his heart toward his God, and perfect in love to God? Is a perfect heart under the all sufficient atonement an impossibility? If so, then

Jesus Christ cannot save unto the uttermost, and His blood cannot cleanse from all sin.

3. Perfect love implies that love is the ruling passion of the believer, the spring of all his energies, and the controlling motive to duty. "The love of Christ constraineth us." Love governs the will, rules the life, dominates the desires, controls the purposes, and sits a queen upon the heart's throne. Duty is now discharged, not so much because it is duty, though the believer never reaches a state where the sense of obligation is absent. But duty is discharged largely because love prompts it. He serves the Lord not because he must do it, but because he loves to serve Him.

"For what are outward things to thee,
  Unless they spring from love?"

"Serve the Lord with gladness." Perfect love renders a service to God ungrudgingly, uncomplainingly, without inward reluctance. Cheerfulness in the service of God is now the predominating feature of the life. What is done for God is done gladly, lovingly, joyfully, not with a secret indisposition to do it.

"Labor is rest and pain is sweet,
  If thou, my God, art there."

"I delight to do thy will, O my God." Perfect love does not shrink at self-denial and sacrifices for its Lord. Crosses are readily taken up and toil becomes a pleasure.

The perfected believer finds "His commandments are not grievous," and "His yoke is easy and the burden is light."

O how great the need of perfect love just at this time in the Church of God if this statement of this grace is correct! How much service is rendered in which there is heartlessness, complaining, reluctance, and the absence of anything like love as the inspiration of it! How little service is rendered which springs from a heart filled with love! What a weariness is much of the service seen in the Church! How cold and dead is much that is done! How unlike the man described in the Psalms: "Blessed is the man that feareth the Lord, that delighteth greatly in his commandments!"

4.   Perfect love implies complete deliverance from all "fear which hath torment."

There are several branches to this fear:

First, all *slavish fear of God* is cast out, and the heart is now filled with the filial fear of God. The perfected believer is not afraid of God, though he reverences Him and fears Him too much to sin against Him, but he does not dread God as before. He does not look at God as one who proposes to punish him, but he thinks of Him as the Holy One who will surely reward him for his faithfulness. He is now moved by love for God, not by a slavish fear. He is no longer a slave, trembling as in the presence of a dread autocrat, but rests consciously in the favor of God as his Father in heaven.

Secondly, all *fear of want* is cast out, simply because a perfect faith in the Divine Providence has come in. He does not fear he will starve, nor is he afraid he will become poverty-stricken, and die in the poor house. He rests securely in the promise, "Bread shall be given him; his waters shall be sure." He takes no anxious thought for the morrow about what he shall eat and what he shall drink, for his faith rests in the God who numbers his hairs and cares for the sparrows.

Thirdly, *fear of man* is cast out. "The fear of man bringeth a snare," and this sort of fear no longer dominates him and makes him miserable when duty comes up for a decision. He is not afraid of what men may say nor think of him so long as God is pleased with his way of living. This is the meaning of that "boldness" of which we read in the Acts of the Apostles, which possessed the early disciples. They were bold to speak the word of God, not fearing the face nor threatenings of men, simply because they had been delivered from the "fear which hath torment." And so it is today with those made perfect in love.

Fourthly, the *slavish fear of death* is cast out. Not that the believer now wants to die, and prefers death to life. In every heart there is the desire to live. No state of grace makes one careless about living. But perfect love makes one ready to die or live, and fully delivers him from that dread of death which harasses many good people, which keeps them in bondage, and which disturbs their minds when death comes before them. "And deliver them who, through fear of death, were all their lifetime subject to bondage."

Lastly, *all fear of evil* is cast out. That is, those vain imaginings of impending evil, the fear of something coming which is calamitous, the fears which ever and anon arise to distress the mind, when there is no real cause for them. These fears do not always take definite shape, but are often like a mist or fog, which cloud the brain and darken the spiritual sky. In Proverbs it is written, "They shall be quiet from the fear of evil." Mark the expression. Not safe from *the evil*, but quiet from *the fear* of it. It is deliverance from the fear of what is coming, no matter what comes in the providence of God. It is quietness of mind from the dread of anything which lies ahead of us, because "sufficient unto the day is the evil thereof."

This, then, is perfect love. What objection can mortal man have to it? Is it not desirable? Would it not make men better if they possessed it? Wherein would it harm any one? Why, then not seek it with all your heart?

SERMON IX.

A VISION OF CHRIST.

Evangelist J. B. Kendall.

"Behold the Lamb of God, which taketh away the sin of the world."   John 1:29.

There is no more pathetic figure in the Scriptures than that of the forerunner of our Lord. Lonely and ascetic, charged to fight against all the social orders, seeing many of his disciples leave him for another master. Then changing the free wilderness for a prison cell, and finally murdered, the victim of a profligate woman's hate and a vicious man's perverse sense of honor.   But perhaps most pathetic of all is the combination in his character of gigantic strength and absolute humility.   How he confronts these people whom he had to rebuke, and yet how, in a moment, the flashing eye sinks in lowest self abasement before "Him that cometh after me."

Christ was a parabolical preacher, He represented heavenly things by familiar similitudes; so John takes that metaphorical description of Jesus. Nature, which is the handiwork of God, has its beauties which are wholly unappreciated by the one who is born without taste for them.   They are

A Vision of Christ. 85

as indifferent to the beauties of a lovely landscape
as are the cattle that browse on its bosom.

Again, nature's beauties often disappoint its
warmest admirers. Such disappointment awaits
none who get a vision of Christ. We look with
amazement upon nature's magnificent grandeur,
unable to describe in words what our eyes behold.
If this be true of nature: if the most glowing language of prose or poetry can do no justice to its
scenes, what words can set forth a "Vision of
Christ."

"Put an angel or a seraph in the pulpit and give
him Christ for his theme. The subject is greater
than his power, the flight above his wings, the
song above his compass. He would be the first to
say when called upon to describe the glories and
beauty, ths majestic and mercy that meet in Jesus:
who is sufficient for these things"? He in whom
heaven and earth, angel and men are perfectly
joined. Yea! you might listen all your life time
to no other theme and on arriving in heaven you
would exclaim with rapt astonishment borrowing
the words of Sheba's Queen: "I had heard of Thee
in mine own land, of Thy acts and thy wisdom;
and behold the half was not told me." In presenting this theme I do not pretend to do justice
to Christ. I only attempt to do you good by di-
recting you to Him.

1. *Behold the Lamb of God With the Father.*

Christ was with the Father from the beginning,
with him in creation, with him in the plan of re-

demption. He was the Lamb slain from the foundation of the world. He descended from the highest heights to the lowest depths and touched every phase of our human nature. He had a higher and more royal origin than Bethlehem's manger. Was of nobler parentage than Mary. Of an older and more regal ancestry than Juda's King.

"The lowly spring that wells up among the willows of the valley has its source in those lofty eternal snows whose spotless bosom bears no stain or print of human foot," so it was with Christ. It is no disgrace to be born of humble parentage. Jesus recognized Mary and honored her as His mother in His dying hour. Yes! the Son of God assumed our nature and descended to save the world. What a descent! How immeasurable the distance between the throne of the eternal and the stable of Bethlehem, the bosom of God and the breast of Mary.

Hear how He might have spoken of Himself:—

"I was the Almighty's chief delight,
    From everlasting days;
Ere yet His arm was stretched forth,
    The heavens and earth to raise.

"Before the sea began to flow,
    And leave the solid land,
Before the hills and mountains rose,
    I dwelt at His right hand."

There are depths of ocean man never sounded;

there are heights in the blue heavens that were never stirred by an eagles' wing; there are regions of truth which angels have never explored, which their eyes never scanned, and where their feet never trod; and such, the deepest of all doctrines, the profoundest of all mysteries, the strangest of all our confidences, is this, that He who expired on Calvary was not the creature, nor, as men and angels are, created, but the eternal Son of God.

2. *Behold the Lamb of God as the sinners' friend.*

To an awakened sinner's ear there is no music on earth, nor in the golden harp of heaven, like the name of Jesus. There is an ointment in its meaning, fragrant as the spikenard of the alabaster box; "His name is as ointment poured forth." If His name is such a blessed thing, what must the sight of Him be? To see Jesus clearly with the eye of faith is to see the deep opening away from Egypt's shore; the water gush, sparkling from the desert rock; the serpent gleaming on its pole over the dying camp of Israel; the blind receive their sight, the lame walk and deaf hear; is to see a pardon when the noose is over our neck and our foot is on the drop. No sight in the wide world like Jesus Christ .

He whose beauty attracts all heaven, whose presence fills all space, whose love comforts and gladdens the troubled heart, has been the central figure of the universe through all ages. Haggai says He is the desire of all nations. He whose infinite glory exalted Him "far above all principality and power and every name that is named." Sinner, do you behold Him? A vision of Him is a vision of one's self.

Adam, pure from the hands of his maker, clothed with terrestrial glory and celestial beauty, was divested by sin, saw his shame and nakedness in the presence of God, and tried to hide himself.

Young and full of worldly ambition, Jacob left his home to go abroad and make his way in the world. At a vision of Jehovah he saw his undone condition, pledged fidelity to God and resolved to go back to his father's house.

When Saul of Tarsus, that haughty, stiff-necked Pharisee, an iron will, a hand of steel, and a heart breathing out threatening and slaughter, a Roman army at his command, authorized by the Sanhedrin to destroy the disciples of Christ, got a vision of the "Lamb of God," he fell on his face blinded by the glory of that vision, cried out of the depths of his lost soul, "Lord, what wilt thou have me to do?"

The publican and Pharisee went up to the temple to worship. The Pharisee saw no one but himself, while the other under the reflection of the shekinah, smote his breast, and with his face to the ground, said: "God be merciful to me a sinner."

The king of Chaldea in all his pomp and earthly glory, full of blasphemy and adultery, surrounded by a thousand lords, on that memorable night when they were drinking wine with his wives and concubines, caught a glimpse of Jehovah's finger as it recorded his soul's destiny on the wall of that beautiful palace. With flashing eye and smiting knees and horror in his face he cried out of the bitterness of a doomed soul to know the whole truth of the matter, which the man of God revealed, but did not save Belshazzar from his awful fate.

When on the border of despair because of our own failures and the failures of others, so much worldliness, sorrow and vice, a vision of "The Lamb of God" will light up the dull eye and warm the cold heart, because He has borne our sorrows and carried our griefs. If you call upon Him He will answer, and thou canst say, "I know that my Redeemer liveth." Then look on no man any more as the ideal for yourself or the pattern of your life, save Jesus only. The gaze will encourage your hope, inspire your confidence, and so establish you that it will make you a master of every situation and an overcomer of *all sin*. It will turn the tide of life and increase the desire for Him, until you can say with the poet:

"Since my eyes were fixed on Jesus,
   I've lost sight of all beside;
So enchained my spirit's vision,
   Looking at the Crucified."

3. *Behold the Lamb of God as our sanctifier.*

"The Lamb of God that taketh away the sin;" here we have two definite articles, *The Lamb* of God and *The sin*.

"For the bodies of those beasts whose blood is brought into the sanctuary by the high priest for sin are burned without the camp. Wherefore Jesus (The Lamb of God) also that he might sanctify the people with his own blood, suffered without the gate." Heb. 13:11-12. Follow Him from heaven on His mission. He was oppressed and He was afflicted, yet He opened not His mouth; He was "brought as a *Lamb* to the slaughter." Isa. 53:7.

He was an outcast from human sympathies, many doors He sought were shut in His face. Did a man ever utter a more touching word than this: "The foxes have holes, and the birds of the air have nests, but the Son of man hath not where to lay His head"? These sorrows were but muttering thunder, the first big drops that precede the bursting of the storm, it came roaring on; and would you see the Lamb of God, in the great sacrifice, for THE SIN, look here; pass into the garden; draw near with reverent steps; He prays in agony; prostrate on the ground; He is sweating as it were great drops of blood. Follow the prisoner to the judgment hall; blood streaks His face, trickling from a crown of thorns, the mocking wreath sin wove for His royal brow, "The crown of which his mother crowned him in the days of his espous-
"   Go out with Him to the street; He faints;

His sacred head lies on the hard stone, but not so hard as pitiless hearts. With the procession pass into Calvary; they cast Him roughly on the ground; they nail Him to the cross, and now it rises slowly over the surging crowd that rend the astonished air with shouts and yells of triumph, "Crucify Him, Crucify Him." See the cloud of desolation deepening, see the blood of redemption streaming ,the tide of life departing as the glaze gathers on His eyes and the awful cry, loud and clear, in the still darkness; My God, My God, why hast thou forsaken me? Then with the last departing breath exclaimed, *"It is finished!"* and thus He, by the grace of God tasted death for every man, Heb. 2:9, and opened the fountain in the house of David for sin and uncleanness, Zach. 13:1.

This was what Isaiah saw when he beheld the Lord high and lifted up. In whose presence he saw his own uncleanness. He unreservedly acknowledged the truth and openly confessed his need. He did not merely assent to it, that it was the doctrine of his church and every one ought to have it, and go on rejecting it, but, like Paul in Rom. 7:24, "O wretched man that I am," Isaiah said: "Woe is me!" Not because he was not regenerated up to date, but his situation was the same as any other justified soul when, convicted for holiness, he sees the old man; it means to get the experience or forfeit one's justification. Thousands today in all our churches are as fruitless as

the barren fig tree and as lifeless as an Egyptian
mummy because they have trodden under foot
the Son of God and counted the blood of the cov-
enant wherewith they are sanctified an unholy
thing. Isaiah was aware of this fact, and by humble obedience and faith, received the sanctifying
flame that burned out inbred sin. Isa. 6:1-8.

We pass on a few centuries to the Mount of
Transfiguration. Here the veil was rifted and humanity was entranced in the presence of glorified
saints, while Moses and Elias bore testimony to
the Son of God who was manifested to destroy the
works of the devil. The presence of these two
prophets was very significant. The fact that they
lived with God centuries after their mortality had
seen decay, proved beyond the shadow of a doubt
the efficiency of the great redemptive scheme which
He should accomplish at Jerusalem, of which
they spoke so confidently; and while Moses and
Elias represented the law and the prophets, mul-
tiplied thousands were filling heaven with praises
to Him who had been slain from the foundation
of the world.

This great fountain which began to be discover-
ed to public view by John the Baptist and poured out in a mighty current on the day of Pentecost through Jesus Christ, its channel and living
head, sanctified the early church, through which
it has flowed on down to the present time, bearing
testimony all along the way to the cleansing power
of the blood and crying to a thirsty multitude and

a sin cursed world: "If any man thirst let him come unto me and drink." John 7:37

While the witnesses we have mentioned were Old Testament saints, we mention one under the New, and thus prove the efficiency of the atonement down to the present time. Stephen, full of the Holy Ghost, spake with such spirit and wisdom in the presence of a corrupt ecclesiasticism and a gainsaying world that they became enraged and with one accord rushed on him with stones. While murderous hands sent a fatal missile that crushed the life out of the first martyr of Christianity he looked beyond "this veil of tears" as the indwelling Christ shone out of his face with a heavenly lustre. Suddenly the gate of heaven swung open to receive his redeemed soul, and the first thing that attracted his longing vision was *the Lamb of God,* standing at the right hand of the Father. He was soon to be delivered from the slavery of the flesh to bask in celestial splendor, amid walls of jasper, gates of pearl and streets of gold in the light and love of eternal glory, with countless millions of saints out of every nation and kindred, and tongue, and people, and loved ones gone before, who have come out of great tribulation with their robes washed and made white in the blood of the Lamb.

SERMON X.

THE DANGER IN NEGLECTING SALVATION. AN APPEAL TO THE SINNER.

Evangelist H. W. Bromley.

"Strive to enter in at the strait gate: for many, I say unto you, will seek to enter in, and shall not be able." Luke 13:14.

There are always two sides to a man's salvation. There is a sense in which he saves himself. And then there is a far more important sense in which he is saved by another. God has so constituted things that in man lies the power of his salvation or ruin.

We are told that Jesus "came not to judge, but to save." And on the other hand it is said that we should 'save ourselves from this untoward generation,' and that by 'taking heed unto ourselves and unto the doctrine we shall save ourselves.'

The Scriptures declare that Christ "came to seek that which was lost," and yet they urge that the sinner "seek the Lord while he may be found." Jesus exclaims, "Behold I stand at the door and knock," and at another time exhorts us to 'knock, and it shall be opened to us.' As it is with the words, "save," "seek," and "knock," so it is with

94

the word "strive." "My Spirit shall not always strive with man;" and for that reason he urges the command of the text: "Strive to enter in at the strait gate: for many, I say unto you, will seek to enter in, and shall not be able."

God's seeking the sinner is a matter of gratuity. Man is the offending party, not the Almighty. It is man who has broken, or allows to remain broken, the harmony between God and himself. And if there is any seeking or striving to be done, it certainly lies at the door of the sinner. The obligation is not on God's part. The sinner is to blame, and it is his duty to beg for pardon. God has never treated the transgressor in any but a just and proper way.

The truth is that God is exceedingly good in making provision for man to be recovered from his lost estate. Every man is created with a principle in him that will live on forever. His behavior in this world does not alter this fact; he must live on in another life, somewhere, whether he wills or not. His attitude, however, toward God in this life, determines his state of existence in the life to come. And there can be but two separate and distinct states for the immortal soul to live in in the life to come. One of those is bounded by God's love and mercy, tributes of the highest, best, and most well-rounded existence. The other must be its opposite: a realm of hatred and inclemency, lawlessness and disorder, supreme misery, and stagnated development, and lacking in all those elements that invariably accompany the better existence.

God is working out the destiny of the universe. Every fully saved man is in harmony with His plans and purposes. But the sinner is out of God's order. He is not in touch with the great march of eternal events which is headed toward the destiny of all things good. The sinner's way is disordered. No matter what method he employs and how arduously he applies himself, being outside the inward workings of the divine plans, he can but reap the wrong eternal results.

The urgency of the Bible in the matter of the sinner's salvation does not rise out of an arbitrary rule of the Almighty. There are too many ways in which the matter is too closely related to the welfare of the sinner. It is to the sinner's advantage to seek the salvation of his soul.

He has unawakened powers within him that, when aroused by divine grace, are capable of producing a character of happiness, adaptability, and usefulness that he does not now dream are possible for him.

The call of God is for the sinner's good. And yet many a transgressor discovers it to be a struggle, not only to surrender, but to make up his mind to surrender, to God. The reason of this lies in the strength of sin. His main fight is with his will, which has been weakened by, and prejudiced in favor of, sin. He has to battle with his carnal self, with its overgrown desires, inclinations, pro-

pensities, and habits. His next struggle is with
a semi-congenial world. His associations must be
reckoned with. Man is a social creature, and it is
natural that men should seek the company of
others with whom they agree, whose likes and dis-
likes are similar to their own. And they then
drift into one another's way of thinking and doing until their habits and desires are confirmed,
and they are firmly fixed in a realm bounded by
certain common ties. While each sinner may not
enter into and become attached to every trans-
gression of his associates, and may even object to
certain of their sins or habits, yet he is committed
to their plane of life. He has not known, or does
not now know, a higher, and is so enthralled in
these chains that it would mean to him a struggle
to break loose, and throw himself into a better
life.

And then again, having so long been adapted
to the realm of the sinner in thought and general
mental attitude, as well as in physical appetites
and desires, to enter into the Christian life the
average sinner feels that it means not only a decision for a better life, but that it involves such a
change in thought, desire, habit, and companions,
to accomplish which he must so continually and
arduously apply himself that it almost looks to
him like an impossibility under his present circumstances,—and here many a sinner is con-
strained to say, "Not tonight." As a sinner he feels
his adaptability to the plane of the sinner. And

he seems to feel that should he become a Christian, he would be lifted into the realm of the Christian, with none of the attributes of the Christian, but with all the old desires, inclinations, and habits which are so closely associated with and are adapted to the life of the sinner. Hence, he feels that there would be a kind of loneliness and dissatisfaction resulting from his present surrender to God. He thinks that religion is all right, and expresses his hope that some day he may become a Christian, but not now. It does not occur to him that, if Christianity is a sad, lonesome religion now, it is likely never to be less so, and that if it is ever to be valuable, it is now.

The average sinner seems to be imbued with the thought contained in the scriptural statement that the Christian life is a narrow way. The Bible is right—it always is. This life is "a narrow way." It narrows the soul down to doing right. And right is always best for any man, physically, mentally, or morally. The whole attitude of the sinner is wrong, and mixing right with wrong does not make wrong right. It is a great mistake to suppose that the wrong doer, with the privilege of adding as much good to his life as he desires, has a broader realm for his activities than he who does right alone. The narrow way is gloriously broad enough to completely satisfy every longing of the humal soul. Is not that enough? What more does the sinner want?

Let me say, with all possible emphasis, that

sin is in no way, shape, form, style, fashion, or sense necessary to human happiness. Happiness cannot be produced by sin. Happiness is essentially a spiritual quality, depending upon spiritual faculties for its recognition and appreciation. Sin appeals to disorganized conditions, and without its purely physical effects would soon be abandoned by the sinner. Sin's most effective strategy is in appealing to and entertaining the sinner with pleasurable sensations, purely physical, or nearly so, while, unknown and unrecognized by the sinner, a tremendous grip is secured upon his spiritual being. Divorce from sin these so-called pleasures, which are only and always temporary, and the sinner would banish sin from his life forever. Sin is the Brutus who pretends friendship while the dagger is sent to the heart of the spiritual life. It is a Judas embracing with a kiss while the hand contains the price of betrayal.

Another fact that should appeal to the sinner is the statement of Christ: "Few there be that find it." There are multitudes of sinners that never make any effort whatever. A large majority of the remainder only attempt it faintly and indefinitely. A great per cent of those still left seek only once or twice and then give it up. Many of the balance are satisfied with "feeling better," signing a card, being baptized, or joining the Church. Comparatively few sinners ever get really saved.

In the first place, most people die young. Very

few, compared with the immense number born, ever live to be old. To pass the average limit of life is to run a race with death.

The second reason is that the power of sin accumulates with age. Like whiskey, or any other kind of habit, its grip grows as it is engaged in.

Then again, there is in sin a powerful tendency to repetition. And repetition forms the habit, and every sin forges another link in habit's chain. And oh! how hard to break loose from habit!

A fourth reason is that the desires of the flesh become confirmed.

A fifth is that the sinner gets accustomed to gospel preaching.

A final and the most fearful reason is that in his rejection or negligence, the sinner may cross the dead line of the Gospel call, and thus be lost forever.

Oh, sinner, Now is the day of thy salvation! Now is the time of divine visitation. The gospel invitation is offered now, and not to-morrow. To-morrow belongs to God; To-day is only yours, and not all of that. *Now* is your time, and *now* you should surrender to God. You may be saved now, but perhaps you do not see the necessity; you may realize the necessity to-morrow, or sometime, but your doom may then be sealed.

Oh! the danger of that peculiar proneness to defer surrender to God! "Plenty of time yet!" was never spoken by divine permission. God has warned here, and many a soul has tripped into perdition over such a vain hope.

Do not do as did a young lady in a revival meeting one night. The pastor approached her in the audience and earnestly and tearfully entreated her to give her heart to God, warning her of the danger of death and of quenching the Spirit. When he turned away she hastily wrote in the fly-leaf of her song-book the fatal words, "I'll risk it!" and underscored them three times.

Weeks after the meeting closed he stood at her bedside and again broached the question of salvation. She looked at him with fearful and hopeless eyes and cried out, "No, no, it can't be now! I could have been saved that night you spoke to me in the meeting and warned me of my great danger, but I refused, and wrote in my song-book those fatal words, 'I'll risk it!' and the Spirit left me forever! Oh, I'm lost, lost, LOST!"

And thus she died!

Oh! sinner, don't risk it; it is too dangerous, but turn to God to-day!

SERMON XI.

YE MUST BE BORN AGAIN.

Rev. E. A. Fergerson.

"Jesus answered and said unto him, Verily, verily,
I say unto thee, Except a man be born again he
cannot see the Kingdom of God." Jno. 3:3.

I suppose every one expects to get to heaven
sometime. There is no one who does not cherish
this fond hope in his heart at some time or other.
Man is born into this world with a nature in him
that worships something; hence the importance of
getting men to worship the true God. On every
hand we find people who trust in their creeds,
doctrines and modes of worship rather than in
God Himself. I often look at this text and think
how pathetically Jesus must have looked on Nicodemus when He said to him, *"You must be born
again."*

Salvation from heaven can only come through
the new birth. Of the six hundred religions ex-
tant in the world to-day, none of them proposes
to save a man from all sin and give him eternal
life, except the religion of Jesus Christ. Who
would think of saying, "He that hath Buddha
hath eternal life," or, "He that hath Mohammed
hath life?" No one of course! But when we

come to the Bible it says, *"He that hath the Son hath life."*

Now if we are ever born of the Spirit there must of necessity come a crisis in our life. Christians are not turned like broom-handles out of a factory, they are born. This very word pre-supposes life. There can be no life without first contact with the same. God only is the author of life, hence a man must be born from above, or, in other words, be born of God. The promise is that when Zion travails sons and daughters will be born. The Holy Spirit will bring on this crisis and work such a conviction in the soul that there will be no rest day nor night till the work is accomplished. When people get to where they cannot sleep or eat, or have any rest, and their hands turn cold, and they feel like they are going to die and hell is their portion if God does not save them, *then* they begin to understand what the pangs of repentance are, and cry out for God to save them. God alone must do the work. He *only* can convict, regenerate, sanctify, etc.

Thank God, He *can be found!* In the day you seek Him with your *whole heart* He will be found of you. He is still in the saving business. Every man and woman in this wicked world who is living in sin is there by choice, and over the protest of the Holy Spirit. We may fail to be true to each other, but the Holy Spirit will prove faithful to all. He is in this world reproving men of sin and judgment. Now since men are free agents and not machines, they have the power of choice, hence God says, *"Choose ye this day whom ye will serve."* God will *convict* men against their wills, but He will never *save* them against their wills. Thank God there is such a thing as getting into the sweat-box of conviction and obtaining a case of old-fashioned, back-woods' religion that will knock sin and the devil out of a person's heart. Brother, you need it, and I am here to tell you that you can get it. Hallelujah! You may have to sweat, but you can get it. This eternal life is what people want above everything else and they are doing the least to obtain it.

There is as much difference between the religion of Jesus Christ and the popular religions of this world as there could be between a rock and a live plant. Although they have much in common, yet the plant possesses something above and beyond and so very different from that of the rock that there could be no way of comparison whatever. Now, what is that something? It is the principle of *life.* Mr. Herbert Spencer, the eminent scientist, says, "If in the natural world we had perfect environment, we should have perpetual, or everlasting, life.' To this Mr. Darwin and Mr. Huxley both agree. While it is true that in the natural world we have not perfect environment, yet in the spiritual we have. *God* is the environment of the child born from above, for *"in Him we live and move and have our being."* This is why the Scriptures tell us in the words of Jesus, *"He that be-*

lieveth on me shall never die, and again, *"He that believeth on me, though he were dead, yet shall he live."* This is an old-fashioned and stern theology that says the sinner is dead in trespasses and sins, also, *"Ye that were dead He hath quickened,"* yet again, *"She that liveth in pleasure is dead while she liveth."*

But the sinner may be translated out of darkness into light, out of death into life. Just as the mineral kingdom is sealed against the animal, so the natural man is sealed against the Spirit of God. Spiritual things are foolishness to the natural man for he cannot understand them. It is a moral impossibility, on the same principle that he who is not born from above *cannot* see the kingdom of God.

The constituent elements of the natural body are oxygen, hydrogen, carbon and nitrogen, with a mixture of iron, lime, soda, phosphates, etc., and we seek food of the same elements to sustain us. The constituent elements of the spiritual man are love, joy, peace, goodness, gentleness, meekness, faith, etc., and in God, our perfect environment, we find all the above elements to sustain the spiritual man.

The nearest thing some folks have to religion, is the rag doll profession. Thank God, brother, you can have the real live baby experience. Not the rag posey, but the real geranium. No wonder poor old Nicodemus wanted to know something of it, as he was a stranger to the real salvation of

Jesus. If you are ever born, and born alive, you will come a-squalling. Hallelujah! Folks will know you are around; they will begin to ask questions and want you to explain. Well, brother, it is not explainable, but it is gettable, haveable, liveable and satisfiable. Glory to God!

Now we have a great over-grown crop of people in this country who are trying to get to heaven by good works. Yes, and do you know that ever since Cain killed Abel we have had two kinds of religion in this world—a religion of works and a religion of faith. The Book says that if you try to climb up some other way than has been laid down in the word you are a thief and a robber. God has not one way of saving one crowd of folks in this country and another way of saving some other crowd. No sir! If you would see heaven, "ye *must* be born again."

This is a free country, and we are all doing the things we want to. If a man wants to shake off conviction and say no to God he can do so. If a man prefers to live in sin and burn incense to passion, and give himself up to the lusts of the flesh, he may do so. In spite of the warnings of God, and the sermons and exhortations of men, the admonitions and prayers of loved ones, the sweet influences of the Gospel, I say in spite of all that has been done to save men, they *can* make their bed in hell.

On the other hand a man can go to heaven, in spite of all the devils in hell or out of it. The devil's gang can rear around, and curse, and blow smoke in his face, and paw the dirt, and bellow, but in spite of the whole thing he can shout and sing and pray and go on to heaven with victory in his soul. Hallelujah!

Now the truth is, you are either saved or you are not, one or the other. You are born from above, or you are still in your sins, and if you are still in your sins you are as dead to the religion of Jesus Christ as a post. This plant called eternal life is exotic. It does not naturally grow in this country, but it will grow if set out in the right kind of soil. When you are regenerated everlasting life is infused into the soul. When you are *sanctified* eternal death (sin) is pulled up by the roots and the dirt is shaken off over old Adam's grave and the holes filled up with everlasting joy, and you go on to heaven with victory in your soul. Now I am talking directly to people who are strangers to the religion of Jesus Christ, although at the same time they have their names enrolled on church records, and if they should die their pastor would preach them to heaven, when the truth is they are not fit for heaven, and they feel that they are not.

I tell you folks now-a-days are trying to find an easy way to heaven, but they will never find it. No one has ever yet obtained a patent right on religion, that is, the Bible kind. Neither has any one run a trust on it. Some have tried in the last five years, but they have miserably failed.

The devil has bamboozled a lot of folks and they have swapped off their pure gold for a lot of old brass.

The real thing will make a man straighten up his back tracks and live right. You will be the husband of only one wife and you will love her better than some other man's wife. You will pay your honest debts, and quit lying, and stealing, either in the day light or after dark. In fact you will make the crooked places straight, the low places high, and the high places low. And I am here to tell you that if the love of the world is in you the love of the Father is not in you. Then you say, Brother Fergerson, according to that kind of preaching there will only be a very few people get to heaven. That's exactly what my Bible says. In Matt. vii. 13, it says, *"Few there be that find it."* Brother, it will cost you something to get right, but it will cost you your soul in hell if you do not get it the right way.

If the needle varies a thousandth part of an inch, the vessel will come short of the desired haven, and if you do not start right in this voyage you will come out wrong.

The philosophy of the truth of the text is seen all through the Word of God. Listen! *"Do men gather grapes from thorns?"* No! No more than one can be alive and dead at the same time. It not only is a moral impossibility, but it is a scientific impossibility for one to be dead and alive at the same time.

Again. *"Do men gather figs of thistles?* Never!

Does a stream send forth fresh and salt water at the same time and place? *"What fellowship hath light with darkness?" "What concord hath Christ with Belial?" None!* Brother, if you are saved at all, you are saved from *all* sins, or you are not saved from any sins. God does not save the people by halves or three-quarters, or eight-ninths or nine-tenths. He saves you from *all* sin. John says, *"Herein are the children of God and the children of the devil manifest."* One crowd sins and the other does not. "Whosoever is born of God doth not commit sin." It is impossible to be a child of God and at the same time sin. Just as a grain of corn cannot grow when it is out of the right relation (out of the earth), so, a man out of the right relation with God (in sin) can never have eternal life.

If you sin you are a child of the devil. Now, I thank God for something that puts a stop to the sinning business, and sweetens life and puts a new song in your mouth, even praises to God. Thank God, I have that song. Should some folks lose their religion they would be none the wiser. Thank God for something that keeps the every day life sweet, keeps you in the dark places, and the easy places, and in the low places, blessed be God, and puts a hope of glory in you, even eternal life. If any man is a saint he has eternal life, and if he is not a saint, he has not. You can have Jesus Christ in your soul, and He will bring eternal life in your heart, and take away the darkness, and He will help you. He will bind up the broken hearted.

Brother, sister, in the name of Jesus, come and seek Him, and get what I have in my soul, and I tell you as a man, without any excitement, it's the best thing on earth; it's the thing we need in our homes, and the thing we need in our places of business, in the   thoroughfares and in every walk of life. I do praise God that Jesus has condescended to come into my life, and is dwelling in my soul, and this new life has come in. When I walk the streets, I get happy. Just to think, I will never die. Heaven is my home, God is my Father, Jesus my elder brother, and I will never die, for He said, "He that believeth on me shall never die." I do bless God for this old-fashioned religion that saves a man through and through.   There are churches and schools and great congregations of people that do not believe in this. Well, if they will bring out something that gives more peace,   more rest and quietness into our lives than we have, we will listen to them. But not until then will we listen for a moment; we will hold on to what we have. This is the thing that this old world is dying for.   You can be saved, you can find God. Jesus Christ is in this audience, in this very room. He will take away the sin, He will come in, and make His abode in your soul, glory be to God, and you can walk out into the world a child of God, and a joint heir with Jesus Christ. Who will be the first to come?

Sermon XII.

PENTECOST AND ITS RESULTS.

By Rev. G. W. Ridout.

"And they were all filled with the Holy Ghost."
Acts 2:4.

There have been three great epochs in the plan
of redemption. Sinai stands for one, where the
Law was given. Calvary stands for another, where
the Atonement was effected, bringing rebellious
man into an at-oneness with God. Pentecost
stands for another, when the Holy Ghost was be-
stowed upon the Church. Each of these epochs
has its parallel in Christian experience. Like Bun-
yan's pilgrim, we must all have our Sinai, where
we are made to feel the terrors of the law through
a pungent conviction for sin. We find no peace
till we come in sight of Calvary and there at the
cross we are reconciled to God, forgiven and pardoned—this is our conversion. Next it is our
glorious privilege to move on to Pentecost, where,
as a definite work, subsequent to conversion, we
may be filled with the Holy Ghost. Every Christian may have a personal Pentecost. We make a
tremendous mistake when we fail to tarry for it.
Our text is associated with a people who waited

for it and were "filled with the Holy Ghost." The results of this Pentecostal bestowment were wonderful. Among them we may mention:

First. The difference in Christian experience. Before Pentecost there were many things existing in the Disciples that were wrong and decidedly detrimental to the spread of the Gospel. There was strife, worldly ambition, self-seeking spirit, bigotry. There was little "perfect love." Pentecost made an end of this, however. They were made to be "all with one accord." They had all things common. They had singleness of heart. They had received the "fire touch" which burned away their sin, made them pure, gave them power.

Second. The stir it made among the people. Nothing excites a people so much as a revival born of the Holy Ghost. A religion that does not create a stir among the ungodly is not of the Pentecostal order. All Jerusalem was stirred over a little company of Christians getting the Holy Ghost. The same power is needed to move people today.

Third. The conviction it wrought upon the unsaved. Seeing such a wonderful display of the Spirit of God, hearing such words of power from the Spirit-baptized preacher, the onlookers and curious and transgressors were made to cry out, "Men and brethren, what shall we do." Here was a cry of conviction for sin, of deep, intense, spirit-wrought concern of soul. Among those who uttered this cry were some who had taken a part in the

murder of our Lord. Some who had come to
mock were now moved to pray. The scene was
one of holy consternation. Now the prophecy concerning the Holy Ghost was fulfilled. He had
convicted these people of sin, of righteousness, of
judgment.

Fourth, The great ingathering of souls. There
can be no conviction or conversion of the unsaved
unless the Spirit is poured out. The futility of
many modern revival efforts is due to the absence
of the Spirit's baptism. The Holy Ghost fell on
this occasion, purifying and empowering believers
and convicting and converting the unsaved. Three
thousand were converted. What an ingathering!
It could not be otherwise, because the Holy Ghost
had been poured out upon the Church. Let the
same thing happen to us, let the Holy Ghost be
given to the Church, let Him have the right of
way to work, unhindered by preacher or people,
and like results will follow nowadays. Many will
be convicted—many will be truly saved. The
Church will be blessed with the largest ingathering.

Fifth. The ideal type of Christianity begotten
by this Pentecostal bestowment was truly remark-
able. Surely in this early Church Christ must
have seen the "travail of His soul" and was satisfied. See how they walked, continuing "stead-
fastly in the apostles' doctrine and fellowship and
in breaking of bread and in prayers," "praising
God and having favor with all the people."

Sixth. The secret of the Spirit-filled life. "Be filled with the Spirit," comes the exhortation to all believers. "They were all filled with the Holy Ghost," written of the disciples, shows the blessed possibility of such an experience. The Spirit's in-filling brings with it a new conception of the religion of Jesus. It brings with it that unction of the Holy One. It gives the secret of constant victory over self and sin, and makes the believer's life one of "righteousness, peace and joy in the Holy Ghost." It renews, inspires, quickens, inten-sifies. As such it was to Bishop Hamline, when it came upon him as a "holy, sin-consuming ener-gy," and a host of God's people have found by entering into this blessed life peace has supplanted worry, victory has taken the place of de-feat and failure, joy has superceded gloom, light has made darkness flee, and love has driven fear away.

O the Spirit-filled life! Is it thine, is it thine?
Is thy soul wholly filled with the Spirit divine?
O thou child of the King, has He fallen on thee?
Does He reign in thy soul, so that all men may see
The dear Savior's blest image reflected in thee?

.

www.ingramcontent.com/pod-product-compliance
Lightning Source LLC
Chambersburg PA
CBHW021201020426
42331CB00003B/155